A STREAM OF
TRITT

The Collected Correspondence

GW00602052

RALPH TRITT

TRITT Inc.

First published in Great Britain in 2002 by
TRITT Inc.
P.O. Box No. 32703, London W14 0XD

Special thanks: Nick Bryant and Peter White

ISBN 0-9543396-0-6

A catalogue record for this book is available from the British Library.

Photographs by kind permission of Michael Winner et al

Maggi Cock Soup© 1997 Société des Produits Nestlé

Designed, printed and bound in Great Britain by
Storm Media Ltd.

For Jean and Frances

CONTENTS

PROLOGUE

16 Sinclair Gardens,
London
W14 0AT

Most Reverent George Carey,
Archbishop Of Canterbury,
Lambeth Palace,
London
SE1

17th January, 2000

Dear Mr. Carey,

Although my wife and I are both God fearing people, I am afraid we are not regular church goers and are both very confused about the millennium and the whole business of the second coming. Is it due this year or will it now be 2001 as is increasingly looking the case? I know a lot of people have said that 2000 is really the last year of the old millennium and not the first one of the new, so it looks as though they are right.

Do you know what form it will take if it is next year and what we can expect to see? Will it be anything like the eclipse? I expect you are sworn to secrecy but it would be good if it could happen at the Dome, which has apparently turned out to be a bit of a disaster. (Luckily my wife and I don't do the lottery).

Best wishes,

Ralph Tritt

The Revd Canon Colin Fletcher
Chaplain to the Archbishop of Canterbury

Mr R Tritt
16 Sinclair Gardens
LONDON W14 0AT

26 January 2000

Dear Mr Tritt,

I have been asked to write on behalf of the Archbishop to thank you for your recent letter to him.

In answer to your question the return of Christ is not governed by a particular calendar date and none of us know exactly when he will return. In the meantime he calls upon us to prepare for that return by living our lives in the way he would wish us to.

Yours Sincerely,

Colin Fletcher

POLITICAL TRITT

ONE

16 Sinclair Gardens,
London
W14 0AT

Frank Dobson,
Labour Candidate For London Mayor,
Houses Of Parliament,
London
SW1

14th January, 2000

Dear Mr. Dobson,

Just a few lines to say how much my wife and I support your bid to become mayor of London and how sad we were to hear of the recent setbacks in your campaign against that ghastly man Red Livingstone. We can't believe that you are also behind in the polls to Glenda Jackson, someone who once wrestled in the nude with Oliver Reed who has since died. What a disgrace she is.

If Livingstone did win, and he looks unstoppable, my wife thinks you should be town crier instead. She thinks you've got the right build for the costume and the beard as well. I don't know what you think about that for an idea, but I think you would look good in a tricorn hat with a hand bell and it would mean that you could still have your say.

Anyway, I hope you don't mind me writing like this. I know you must be busy but do you do signed photos? I've enclosed an SAE if you do for our collection. It would be great to have you up on the wall with all the others! (Not Livingstone or Jackson).

Good luck! We'll be voting for you!

Best wishes,

Ralph Tritt

From: The Rt. Hon. Frank Dobson, M.P.

HOUSE OF COMMONS
LONDON SW1A 0AA

Mr. Ralph Tritt,
16 Sinclair Gardens,
<u>LONDON, W14 OAT</u>

24 January 2000

Dear Mr. Tritt,

I acknowledge receipt of your letter dated 14 January. My thanks to both you for your wife for your support in my bid to become Mayor of London.

As requested, I attach a signed photograph.

With best wishes.

Yours sincerely,

ENC:

Telephone (020)

16 Sinclair Gardens,
London
W14 0AT

Ken Livingstone MP,
London Mayor In Waiting,
House Of Commons,
London
SW1A 0AA

4th April, 2000

Dear Ken,

As a former transport worker I am delighted that you have decided to stand as an independent candidate.

Although I'm sure the election on 4th May will be a walkover, I also appreciate that these things need paying for and that the money must come from somewhere. I'm concerned, however, about you taking too much cash from that ginger nut Evans who must surely have an ulterior motive. Far better for you to be using your own money (you seem to have plenty of it!) and funds raised by ordinary people like myself who expect nothing in return.

To this end I am in the throes of setting up a sponsored monkey shave at London Zoo. They apparently have their monkeys shaved down in the springtime anyway but the public aren't to know this. I think you will agree it is a novel way of raising funds as well a being a good deal of fun for all those involved. All I need to know is who to make the cheque payable to and where I should send it. Perhaps if the amount is significant I could arrange for one of those giant cheques to be drawn and a photo opportunity? I was thinking of contacting Carlton Television anyway but maybe I should see how it goes first?

Anyway, good luck Ken. Not that you'll need it! I hope I can get a few quid together for you.

Best wishes,

Ralph Tritt

16 Sinclair Gardens,
London
W14 0AT

Ken Livingstone MP,
London Mayor In Waiting,
House Of Commons,
London
SW1A 0AA

18th April, 2000

Dear Ken,

I appreciate that you are a very busy man (never more so than now) but surely you must have people to deal with the post you get from ordinary folk like myself?

I wrote to you a few weeks ago asking for details of where to send contributions to your campaign but have heard nothing to date. More importantly, I want to know who the sum should be made payable to. I don't want to just send money addressed to you care of the House Of Commons in case it falls into the wrong hands and causes a stink.

With all good wishes,

Ralph Tritt

Ken Livingstone MP

HOUSE OF COMMONS
LONDON SW1A 0AA

Ralph Tritt
16 Sinclair Gardens
London W14 0AT

25 April 2000

Dear Mr Tritt

Thank you for your letter of 18 April.

I am very sorry you are still waiting for a reply from my campaign office. Unfortunately we have received so much post that my staff are totally overwhelmed but if you would like to send some money to the campaign, you can either send it to me here at the House of Commons or to Ken Livingstone MP, 3 Hanson Street, W1P 7LJ.

Best wishes.

Yours sincerely

Ken Livingstone

16 Sinclair Gardens,
London
W14 0AT

Ken Livingstone MP,
3 Hanson Street,
London
W1P 7LJ

28th April, 2000

Dear Ken,

Thank you for finding the time in your busy schedule to write back to me.

Unfortunately, my original plan to raise funds for your campaign involving the sponsorship of monkeys being shaved at London Zoo has come to nought. It would seem that the Zoo is obliged to stay neutral in political matters and you can't really blame them for that. However, the good news is that our neighbour Mrs. Edgbaston agreed to be shaved by proxy and a fine time was had by one and all. Perhaps less gratifying is the fact that she was only able to raise £3:78, but I have taken it upon myself to round this figure up from my own pocket.

Please find enclosed a postal order to the value of £5 accordingly. It's not as much as I would have hoped but should provide enough for a couple of liveners at the celebration come Thursday night (if that is not considered a misuse of party funds!).

Best wishes,

Ralph Tritt

Livingstone for London

Livingstone for London
PO Box 20052
London
NW2 5ZH

Dear Friend,

8 August 2000

I am writing to thank you for your contribution towards the costs of my Mayoral election campaign. In total, £709,586 was raised — the majority in thousands of relatively small individual contributions. I was amazed and delighted that so many people responded to the appeal and made an independent candidature possible. I am grateful to all donors, big and small, your generosity helped produce an unprecedented result.

Since the election, I have started to construct a broad-based and inclusive administration which genuinely represents the diversity which makes London such a wonderful city. With the formal transfer of powers to the Mayor and Greater London Authority on 3 July, London regained its right to self-government. I firmly believe that to have meaning, self-government must now deliver real benefits to Londoners. That is what I intend to use the next four years to achieve.

My election expenses came to £389,000 — which means that the campaign raised, in round figures, 45 per cent more than was actually spent during the election.

I am therefore writing to all donors to ask whether you would be willing to have the remaining 45 per cent of your contribution donated to the Livingstone for London Campaign to fund continuing political and re-election campaigning, including the maintenance of a website, publication of a newsletter, research and public meetings. The Campaign will publish audited accounts.

Alternatively, if you wish, 45 per cent of your original contribution can be returned to you.

As you can imagine contacting so many donors is itself an enormous operation and I would very much appreciate your early response by filling in the form below and returning it in the stamped addressed envelope provided.

Thank you again for your support,

Yours sincerely,

Ken Livingstone

Ken Livingstone

Please return this form to: Ken Livingstone, PO Box 20052, London NW2 5ZH.

Please use block capitals.

Name .... Address ....

....

Tel ....

.... Email ....

☐ I would like the remaining 45% of my contribution donated to the *Livingstone for London* Campaign.

☐ I would like the remaining 45% of my contribution returned to me at the above address. Please make cheque payable to ....

Signature... Date...............................

The Truckle Club,
16 Sinclair Gardens,
London
W14 0AT

Lord Archer,
The Old Rectory,
Grantchester,
Cambridgeshire

20th March, 2000

Dear Lord Archer,

I hope you don't mind me dropping you a line now all that mayoral fuss seems to have blown over. Particularly as I understand you to be a man after my own heart, that is to say someone who appreciates the finer qualities of cheese!

I hold the chair of The Truckle Club, a group of cheese enthusiasts originally set up by myself along with a few like-minded colleagues from work at London Underground. Having recently taken early retirement (thirty years down the line!) I now have more time to focus on the club's activities and to this end have decided to write to a few celebrity big cheeses like yourself!

Although it is our wish to eventually expand membership beyond the environs of Tube personnel, there are at present eighteen of us. We meet up on a monthly basis and are always on the look out for new or unusual cheese to try at our sessions. I wonder if there is one you could recommend, or perhaps you know of a particularly good supplier of an old favourite? I have to say that there is a strong bias amongst us Trucklers towards blue cheese (the stronger the better!) and we don't have much time for all that runny French stuff either.

Would it be too much to ask also for a signed photo? I've enclosed an SAE for your trouble. Are there any other big cheeses you could suggest I write to? I am keen to get as much endorsement as I can in order to help swell membership but men only. This is something we prefer to keep the wives out of!

Good luck with your future endeavours. Nice and cheesy does it!

Best wishes,

Ralph Tritt
Chairman Of The Truckle Club Cheese Board

17

Jeffrey Archer

House of Lords

Mr R Tritt
Chairman
The Truckle Club
16 Sinclair Gardens
London W14 0AT

27th March 2000

Dear Mr Tritt,

Many thanks for your letter of the 20th March.

My personal favourite is a superb mature West Country Cheddar which I have been buying each Christmas for many years from Alvis Brothers.

I appreciate your taking the time to write, and am enclosing a signed photograph, as requested.

With best wishes to all in The Truckle Club.

Yours sincerely

Jeffrey Archer

16 Sinclair Gardens,
London
W14 0AT

Nick Brown MP,
Ministry Of Agriculture,
Whitehall Place,
London
SW1

24th April, 2001

Dear Mr. Brown,

I wrote to you some weeks ago now but have had no reply. I appreciate that these are testing times for you and your fellow MAFF men, but surely you must have a minion who can take care of the post? I wouldn't mind but I'd asked for something to put up in the window in support of the farmers and had even taken the trouble to enclose an SAE.

Anyway, I see that you have at last started to implement the vaccine programme I advocated in my letter. Well done on that. The carcass disposal, however, still seems to be causing a bit of a stink. Must they be burnt? Why not just stick them straight into the hole with a good layer of quicklime? It's something I can recommend myself, having used it in the past on dogs with excellent results.

I'm not wasting any more money on stamps, but I would still like something for the window. As I stated before, I am a Hague man but these sort of issues should transcend party politics. I wouldn't want to think that my declaration meant I was being treated any differently.

Yours sincerely,

Ralph Tritt

DEFRA
Department for
Environment,
Food & Rural Affairs

Room 104, 1A, Page Street, London, SW1P 4PQ
Helpline   (0845) 050 4141
Fax   0207 904 6053   Leaflet Answerphone   0207 904 6066
E-mail   Marie.chapman@defra.gsi.gov.uk

Mr R Tritt
16 Sinclair Gardens
London
W14 0AT

Our reference: DWO 9153

Dear Mr Tritt,

09 August 2001

FOOT AND MOUTH DISEASE

Thank you for your letter of 24 April 2001 to Mr Brown about the current Foot and Mouth Disease (FMD) outbreak, to which I have been asked to reply. I apologise for the delay in response, I hope you will appreciate the heavy demands that the outbreak is making on staff resources and that it is not always possible to deal with detailed enquiries on time.

I hope that the series of factsheets we sent to you on 24 April answered some of your queries. In your letter of the same day you asked about carcass disposal. I can assure you that we are looking at all possible safe disposal routes including rendering, incineration, on-farm disposal by burning or burial, and landfill. We liase closely with local authorities and the Environment Agency about the most appropriate course to take in individual cases. We have brought in additional manpower to deal with the logistics of the disposal operation, both from civil and military sources, so as to ensure veterinary staff can concentrate on disease control.

It is no longer regarded as appropriate to use lime in disposing of FMD carcasses, as lime tends to preserve them while natural decomposition kills FMD virus by acidity.

I hope this provides answer to some of your questions and further information on Foot and Mouth Disease is available through the comprehensive and regularly updated DEFRA website (www.defra.gov.uk) as well as the dedicated helpline (0845 050 4141) which is available seven days a week.

Yours sincerely,

pp- *[signature]*

Marie Chapman
FMD Communication Branch
Animal Disease Control

INVESTOR IN PEOPLE

16 Sinclair Gardens,
London
W14 0AT

Boris Johnson MP,
House Of Commons,
Whitehall,
London
SW1

17th June, 2001

Dear Mr. Johnson,

Just a few lines of congratulation, now that the dust has settled, on your famous victory amongst the Henley boat people. What a pity that it couldn't project across the country, and that includes our man Carrington here in Hammersmith And Fulham.

It's a terrible shame for young Billy Hague being all washed up at 40. I wonder what he will do now? They usually end up as MEP's, don't they, like Kinnock, but that seems unlikely in his case. I'm not sure how I stand on Portillo either. I think the press will be like a dog with a squeaky toy if he's elected.

Anyway, here's to you restoring a bit of much needed credibility to the Party. Are you doing signed photographs yet? I would love to have one for my collection if you are and have enclosed an SAE for your trouble.

All good wishes for the future.

Save the pound!

Yours sincerely,

Ralph Tritt

Boris Johnson MP

HOUSE OF COMMONS
LONDON SW1A 0AA

Ralph Tritt Esq
16 Sinclair Gardens
London
W14 0AT

20th June 2001

Dear Mr Tritt,

Thank you so much for your letter of 17th June and for your kind words of congratulation.

I am grateful to you for taking the trouble to write with your comments and I enclose a signed photograph as you request.

Best wishes.

Yours sincerely,

Save the pound is right!

BORIS JOHNSON M.P.

16 Sinclair Gardens,
London
W14 0AT

Human Rights,
Home Office,
50 Queen Anne's Gate,
London
SW1H 9AT

15th October, 2001

Dear Sir/Madam,

I understand that there is no need to apply abroad now for Human Rights and that they are available here, but could you let me know exactly what mine are?

I don't want to go into detail at this stage, but I feel that I am being infringed and would like to take legal action. Does it still mean having to pay a solicitor in the normal way? Also, are there different sorts of Rights for different people? It seems that sometimes people say they have them when they can't get their own way. Is that when they are "inalienable" or is it the other way round?

Lastly, if you win a Human Rights case, do the losers have to give you compensation or would they normally just go to prison?

I'm enclosing an SAE for your convenience. Thank you for your help.

Yours faithfully,

Ralph Tritt

LORD CHANCELLOR'S DEPARTMENT

Human Rights Unit

50 Queen Anne's Gate, London SW1H 9AT

Telephone: 020 - 7273 2166
Facsimile: 020 - 7273 2045

Mr Ralph Tritt
16 Sinclair Gardens
London
W14 0AT

Your reference

Our reference

Date

Dear Mr Tritt

18 October 2001

Thank you for your letter dated 15 October 2001, which was received on the 17 October 2001.

The Human Rights Act 1998 came fully into force on the 2 October 2000. It gives further effect in the UK to the rights contained in the European Convention of Human Rights. It means that all legislation must be interpreted wherever possible, in a way, which is compatible with the Convention rights. And public authorities including courts and tribunals must act in a way, which is compatible with those rights.

The Human Rights Act allows cases involving the Convention rights to be heard by our own courts without the need to take the case to Strasbourg.

The rights apply to everyone and are basic fundamental rights.

It is not necessary to have a solicitor to represent you in order to bring a case. Courts can advise you on the procedure. However it is always advisable to seek legal advice.

Unfortunately, we are not able to take up individual cases. The Citizens Advice Bureaux offer advice and information. Legal Advice Centres may be able to help you take your case forward or alternatively the Community Legal Services link people up with advice providers, including Law Centres and Citizen Advice Bureaux, as well as solicitors. The Community Legal Services helpline is 0845 608 1122

I have enclosed a copy of the Study Guide, which you may find helpful. Page 6 of the Study Guide tells you about the type of remedies available. Further information can be found on our website at www.humanrights.gov.uk

Yours sincerely

Sharon LeCount

16 Sinclair Gardens,
London
W14 0AT

Ann Widdecombe MP,
House Of Commons,
Whitehall,
London
SW1

12th November, 2001

Dear Ms. Widdecombe,

Congratulations on your makeover. I have to say that it's taken years off you, but what a shame you couldn't have had it done before the election. I know you don't have much truck with the business of presentation, but the softer look definitely suits you and might have made all the difference in the polls.

Anyway, I hope we haven't seen the last of you and your no nonsense style in the shadow cabinet. I think Mr. Duncan Smith is going to be all right, but he doesn't seem to have much faith in women and has surrounded himself with a lot of lightweights as far as I can see. The only one I've heard of is this man Letwin, but then that's only because he's famous for cocking up! Worse still, he's the one opposing Blunkett, who seems like a hard-liner but then gives carte blanche to the cannabis resin brigade. Mind you, at least they're toughening up on the asylum seekers now, and who would have thought we'd see that from New Labour. It wasn't so long ago that they were calling William Hague a racist for suggesting the same.

Is it possible to have a signed photo if you've had new ones done? I've enclosed an SAE. I expect you'll be looking to lose a few pounds as the next step. My wife is reading about Carol Vorderman's detox diet in the newspaper at the moment, which seems to work wonders. Mind you, by the sound of it, it's something that's best practised if you live on your own!

Yours sincerely,

Ralph Tritt

From: The Rt. Hon. Ann Widdecombe. M

HOUSE OF COMM
LONDON SW1A 0A

Mr. Ralph Tritt
16 Sinclair Gardens
London
W14 0AT

30 Novem

Dear Mr. Tritt,

Thank you very much for your letter of 12th November.

I am grateful indeed for your kind words as it is always nice to receive a
compliment. You have however made the Carol Vooderman detox diet sound
extremely unappealing and I don't think I shall be giving that one a try any time
soon!

I agree that it is extremely ironic that the Government has adopted the very
same policies which they decried as racist during the Election and it is
unfortunately typical of them

I think it important that we all pull together behind the Leader and to realise that
it always takes a ~~short~~ little while for new appointees in any Cabinet to find their feet.

I am delighted to enclose a signed photograph and I thank you again for taking
the time to write to me.

Yours sincerely,

Ann Widdecombe MP

CONSUMER TRITT

TWO

16 Sinclair Gardens,
London
W14 0AT

Regent Academy,
Department N1,
155 Regent Street,
London
W1R 8PX

26th January, 2000

Dear Sir/Madam,

Further to your advertisement, I would be interested in taking advantage of the demand for poofreaders and look forward to receiving your free information.

Yours faithfully,

Ralph Tritt

THE REGENT ACADEMY

LAUDE DIGNUS

27 January 2000

Mr Ralph Tritt
16 Sinclair Gardens
LONDON
W14 0AT
England

Dear Mr Tritt

Thank you for your request. I am delighted to enclose details of the Academy's career-related home-study courses.

Whether you're looking to earn extra income part-time or start your own business, our courses will provide you with all the information you need to succeed.

Even if you have little or no experience, you'll find Regent Academy courses easy to follow – and that they quickly enable you to start making money from your new career.

You get everything you need straight away

With the Regent Academy, you receive *all* your lessons and your practical assignments when you enrol on your course.

In addition, you receive a complete package of high-quality course materials. This includes: elegant binders for your lessons, an assignment wallet, essential videos plus other materials specific to your chosen course.

You are well looked after

All through your course, you'll receive expert advice and professional guidance from your personal tutor, who is dedicated to helping you achieve the success you want.

What's more, you can take advantage of our Free Advisory Service which offers you personal help and guidance over the phone.

Our magazine, *The Review*, keeps you up to date with articles related to your course,

please read on …

153-155 REGENT STREET LONDON W1R 8PX
TELEPHONE 020 7287 8707 • FAX 020 7287 3348
email info@regentacademy.com
web www.regentacademy.com

REGENT ACADEMY OF FINE ARTS LIMITED
REGISTERED OFFICE: 8 BAKER STREET, LONDON W1M 1DA
REGISTERED NUMBER: 2502592

16 Sinclair Gardens,
London
W14 0AT

Customer Services,
Master Foods Ltd.,
Hansa Road,
Kings Lynn,
Norfolk
PE30 4JE

18th January, 2000

Dear Sir/Madam,

As a keen consumer of your Uncle Ben's range of products I am glad to see that you have not allowed yourselves to be brow-beaten by the politically correct crowd. Unlike the Robertson's Jam people who were forced to withdraw their perfectly harmless golliwog by interfering busybodies. Your smiling Negro reminds me of a happier time spent before the world went completely mad.

I wonder now that the gollies are no longer available whether you do an Uncle Ben's Negro badge? I would love to buy some for my nieces and nephews as a reminder of my own childhood. Would you be so kind as to let me know what they cost or advise of any other Negro merchandise you might have available?

Yours faithfully,

Ralph Tritt

Mr. Ralph Tritt
16 Sinclair Gardens
LONDON
W14 0AT

8 February 2000

Dear Mr. Tritt

Thank you for your most recent letter regarding the availability of Uncle Ben's negro merchandise.

Unfortunately, we have to advise you that although all of our products contain the Uncle Ben's logo (wording) we do not have any promotional merchandise/badges which displays Uncle Ben himself.

However, we have pleasure in enclosing an Uncle Ben's Cook Book for yourself together with some Uncle Ben's pencils for your younger relatives. We have also attached a copy of the Uncle Ben's Story which we hope you find interesting.

Thank you for the interest you have shown in writing to us.

Yours sincerely

MRS. HELEN C. PELL
Customer Care Advisor

National Office, Waltham-on-the-Wolds, Melton Mowbray, Leicestershire LE14 4RS
Registered at the Companies Registration Office, London, England. Registered Number: 636458. Registered Office: 3D Dundee Road, Slough, Berkshire, SL1 4LG

FOR HELP & ADVICE 📞 0800 738800

16 Sinclair Gardens,
London
W14 0AT

English Miniatures,
3 Grove Park,
Mill Lane,
Alton,
Hants
GU34 2QG

19th January, 2000

Dear Sir/Madam,

I understand from a fellow collector that you are about to issue fine art sculptures of figures from Nazi Germany in your Bygone Days series.

If this is the case, I would be particularly interested to receive advance details regarding Adolf Hitler (of course!) and any other leading Shultzstaffel or Gestapo members such as Goebbels, Himmler etc.

Yours faithfully,

Ralph Tritt

English Miniatures
FINE ART SCULPTURE

Mr R Tritt
16 Sinclair Gardens
London
W14 0AT

26th January 2000

Dear Mr Tritt,

With reference to your letter of recent date regarding our products. We will not be producing Nazi figurines now or at a later date. A selection of listings is enclosed of the items we produce.

These are available singly or as collections, which are sent on a approval on a monthly basis. Should two or more items be requested together a prepayment is required, which is fully refundable on return of the goods to this office.

Yours sincerely,

Kate Nash.

3 Grove Park, Mill Lane, Alton, Hampshire GU34 2QG
Telephone: 01420 541424   Fax: 01420 541421

E MINIATURES LTD

Registered No.: 2263592   Registered Office

Directors: P.A.Esser S.A.Esser U.L.Esser J.Bailey

16 Sinclair Gardens,
London
W14 0AT

Head Of Marketing,
Terry's Suchard,
P.O. Box 1767,
Cheltenham
GL50 3ZQ

15th February, 2000

Dear Sir/Madam,

I have an idea for an advertising campaign that I think would be perfect for your Chocolate Orange line.

With the Northern Ireland peace process in constant turmoil, would it not be a great idea to have Gerry Adams and David Trimble posing with a Terry's Chocolate Orange? You could have a slogan like: These two have had their differences in the past, but there's one orange order they both agree on!

Apart from helping with relations from a politics point of view, I think it would make brilliant publicity for yourselves and also tie in perfectly with the Easter theme, if we're quick, which is probably your busiest time.

I've just thought also that you could probably get the Rev. Ian Paisley involved too. You could have him eating a Terry's Chocolate Orange with a slogan like: There's only one thing guaranteed to keep him quiet this Easter! Are you a Terry's Chocolate Orange Man?

I am not a professional and have never done anything like this before. I hope you agree that this would be an original idea and I look forward to hearing from you. I shall also be sending a copy of this letter to myself by registered post as proof.

Yours sincerely,

Ralph Tritt

Ref. No. 59143

MR R TRITT
16 SINCLAIR GARDENS
LONDON
W14 0AT

17 February 2000

Dear Mr Tritt

Thank you for your letter concerning an advertising campaign for Terry's Chocolate Orange.

All our advertising is devised by our Marketing Department using the advice and assistance of a specialist advertising agency and we do not normally use ideas from the general public because of problems of copyright etc. Often several people come up with the same idea, or with slight variations on a theme. This might also be an idea already being worked on by our own teams working many months in advance of the finalised campaign.

However we appreciate the trouble you have taken in writing to us and enclose a gift voucher which can be used to purchase any product from our wide range.

Yours sincerely,

Pauline Clarke
Consumer Care
Enclosed: £2.00

Kraft Jacobs Suchard

Consumer Services
St. George's House, Bayshill Road,
Cheltenham, Glos GL50 3AE
Telephone: 01242 236101   Fax: 01242 284612

16 Sinclair Gardens,
London
W14 0AT

Kentucky Fried Chicken,
32 Goldsworth Road,
Woking,
Surrey
GU21 1JT

20th March, 2000

Dear Sir/Madam,

Being of the older generation, my wife and I are not really accustomed to takeaway food but recently decided to give your lot a go on Shepherd's Bush Green. We were attracted as much as anything by the picture of an old man with a stick you use on your posters and eventually plumped for a Twister meal for two. I have to say that we thought the food was absolutely uneatable and will certainly be coming back again to try the rest of the menu. We would love to know what the eleven herbs and spices are that you use but I expect you have to keep them secret in case of industrial espionage.

Do you do merchandise at all? We would love to have a badge of the old man with a stick. Well done for supporting the oldies! Have you ever thought about doing soup as well? I reckon a nice drop of chicken with some of your corn cobettes in it would go down a treat.

Yours faithfully,

Ralph and Frances Tritt

Tricon
Restaurants International

CC-31558-CA

29 March 2000

Tricon Restaurants International
32 Goldsworth Road, Woking
Surrey GU21 1JT
Tel: +44 (0) 1483 717000
Fax: +44 (0) 1483 717152

Mr R Tritt
16 Sinclair Gardens
LONDON
W14 0AT

Dear Mr Tritt

Thank you for taking the time to contact us regarding your visit to our Shepherds Bush outlet. It is not often that our customers take the time to let us know about the good things that we do and it is welcome news indeed.

To prepare KFC Original Recipe Chicken, we take whole fresh pieces of chicken, sprinkle them with cold water and cover them with the special KFC coating made with the Colonel's secret recipe of 11 herbs and spices. Unfortunately, though, the information is top secret, so we're afraid we are unable to give you an ingredients listing.

We would like to thank you for your suggestion for chicken soup. We have passed these details onto our Technical department for further consideration.

Once again, thank you for your comments and your valued custom.

Yours sincerely

Nina Horobin
Customer Services

Kentucky Fried Chicken (Great Britain) Limited Registered In England No. 967403 VAT Reg. 414021513

16 Sinclair Gardens,
London
W14 0AT

McDonald's Restaurants,
11-59 High Road,
East Finchley,
London
N2 8BR

21st March, 2000

Dear Sir/Madam,

On several occasions over the past few years my wife and I have both discovered an unpleasant green mush attached to the soles of our shoes, more often than not after having first walked it through into our carpet. It has always remained a mystery to us what this substance was until a neighbour recently confirmed it to be discarded gherkin emanating from one of your shops!

My wife and I are of an older generation unaccustomed to takeaway food, especially after all this mad cow business with offal products and mechanically reclaimed meat. We have never tried any of your meals but surely gherkin is an odd thing to be serving up if what I am lead to believe is true? If they are as unpopular with your customers as the pavements would seem to suggest then why not make them optional or, better still, dispense with them altogether?

I have taken the trouble of writing to your head office about this as I think it is something that requires an executive decision. In the meantime my wife and I will be watching very closely where we tread around Shepherd's Bush Green.

Yours faithfully,

Ralph Tritt

31st March 2000

Mr R Tritt
16 Sinclair Gardens
London
W14 0AT

McDonald's

Customer Services Department

Dear Mr Tritt

Thank you for contacting us regarding the gherkins you noticed around your house. I am very sorry to learn of this and the inconvenience experienced.

McDonald's restaurants operate very much as part of the community in which they serve and quite naturally therefore take a pride in the appearance of the local environment.

It is our policy to carry out "litter patrols" whereby members of staff will go out and pick up not only McDonald's packaging but other litter which has been discarded. In addition to this, we also provide waste receptacles both inside and outside our restaurants and the majority of our packaging carries the "tidy man" symbol to remind people to dispose of their litter carefully. McDonald's is today one of the country's leading sponsors of council litter bins.

We believe we share the responsibility for litter with individuals themselves. This is why we support the education of local school, local and community groups across the country by organising litter related competitions, and sponsor a number of nationwide education schemes, including the Tidy Britain Group's National Spring Clean and the Groundwork Trust

I would like to assure you that I have discussed this matter with the restaurant team and I have been assured that extra care will taken when the litter patrols are carried out.

Thank you for contacting us on this matter and allowing me to comment and I do hope that you see an improvement in the future.

Yours sincerely

Rhonda Floyd
Customer Services Manager

16 Sinclair Gardens,
London
W14 0AT

Cock Soup,
Nestles Consumer Services,
P.O. Box 207,
York
YO1 1XY

5th April, 2000

Dear Sir/Madam,

Hoorah for Cock! My wife recently bought some of your soup on spec and I have to declare that it is certainly the best I have tasted. You would never guess that it came from a packet and what excellent value for money too. How many other packet soups are there that give you two good helpings without losing flavour? None that I've tried until Cock. The rest simply don't measure up.

I am keen now to try other varieties of Cock but my wife has so far been only able to find chicken. Surely with such a good product as this there is more to your range? I happen to hold the chair of a group of cheese enthusiasts called The Truckle Club and I can assure you that these days cheese soup of any description is thin on the ground. To discover Cock cheese in a packet would certainly put a smile on all our faces, I can tell you.

Anyway, well done Nestles. It's funny to discover who owns what these days. I had always associated you with that funny milk, but now I must be showing you my age!

Yours faithfully,

Ralph Tritt

Nestlé UK Ltd

YORK YO91 1XY

TELEPHONE (01904) 604604
FACSIMILE (01904) 604534

Mr R Tritt
16 Sinclair Gardens
LONDON
W14 0AT

DIRECT LINE: (01904) 604655

DIRECT FAX: (01904) 603461

YOUR REF:

OUR REF:

0391731A

DATE:

6 April 2000

Dear Mr Tritt

Thank you for your recent call to our careline.

We were pleased to learn how much you enjoy our Maggi Cock Soup. We take great care to ensure that our products are of the highest quality and that they reach the public in first class condition. When we receive comments such as yours we realise that our efforts are more than worthwhile.

We are always pleased when consumers take the trouble to contact us since a great deal of time and effort goes into the manufacture and marketing of all our products. It is gratifying to know from your comments that our efforts are appreciated. We do have some other flavours of soup in the Maggi range, cock is just one of them. Cock is one of a number of flavours including celery, leek, asparagus, chicken and french onion.

Thank you once again for taking the trouble to contact us. We hope that you will continue to enjoy our products in the future.

Yours sincerely

L. Murray

Lorraine Murray
Administration Advisor
Consumer Services

16 Sinclair Gardens,
London
W14 0AT

Peter Jones China,
Dept. Q2D,
P.O. Box 10,
22 Little Westgate,
Wakefield
WF1 1LB

18th April, 2000

Dear Sir/Madam,

Re: Third Reich Fifty-Fifth Anniversary 1945-2000

I understand from fellow collectors that you are about to issue celebration mugs in fine bone china to mark this occasion.

Will it be the usual one-off of Herr Hitler or can we expect something more imaginative this time? I am particularly interested in the slightly more obscure figures. People like Eichmann, Hess and Speer who all too often get neglected. Apart from the usual SS suspects, it would be nice to have a few Gestapo and Luftwaffe faces made available too.

I look forward to receiving advance details and enclose an SAE for your convenience. I am also sending no money now.

Thanking you in advance.

Yours faithfully,

Ralph Tritt
(Uber Alles!)

Peter Jones China

P.O. Box 10, 22 Little Westgate, Wakefield,
West Yorkshire WF1 1LB.
Telephone (01924) 362510 Fax (01924) 290234

20 April, 2000

Mr R Tritt
16 Sinclair Gardens
London
W14 OAT

Dear Mr Tritt,

Further to your letter of the 18th April, we have no plans to commission any commemorative china to mark the anniversary of the Third Reich.

Yours sincerely,

D A Jones (Mrs)

16 Sinclair Gardens,
London
W14 0AT

Brooks Bentley,
Weald Court,
101-103 Tonbridge Road,
Hildenborough,
Tonbridge,
Kent
TN11 9RY

6th May, 2000

Dear Sir/Madam,

Seeing your magnificent jewelled crosses for sale recently in my colour supplement left me wondering whether there is more to your range than just the crucifix. Do you also manufacture Maltese or Iron Crosses as favoured by the Nazis? Good reproductions are so hard to find these days as they are thought by some to be in dubious taste.

I would be very interested to receive further information on such items and, indeed, any other Nazi insignia you might happen to supply. With the fifty-fifth anniversary of the dissolution of the Third Reich almost upon us you might well find there is a serious demand for this stuff.

Yours faithfully,

Ralph Tritt

BROOKS & BENTLEY

Mr R Tritt
16 Sinclair Gardens
London
W14 0AT

10th May 2000

Dear Mr Tritt

Thank you for the interest you have shown in our products.

As we continue to introduce new items and discontinue others which sell out, we generally offer our products through individual media advertisements rather than in a catalogue. It is as the result of responding to one of these that a name will be added to our mailing list. On the basis of this first purchase, customers are then selected to receive personalised notification of forthcoming offers.

As we are unable to add your name to our mailing list at this time, we do hope that we may have the opportunity to serve you in the future.

Yours sincerely

Customer Services Department

Ref: CWARD

Brooks & Bentley Ltd, Weald Court, 101-103 Tonbridge Road, Hildenborough, TONBRIDGE, Kent TN11 9RY
Tel: 01732 834400 Fax: 01732 833910 Registered in England and Wales No. 2675093 VAT Reg. No. GB 565 4234 37

16 Sinclair Gardens,
London
W14 0AT

Bradford Exchange Ltd.,
1 Castle Yard,
Richmond,
Surrey
TW10 6TF

6th, May 2000

Dear Sir/Madam,

Re: Third Reich Fifty-Fifth Anniversary 1945-2000

Am I right in understanding that you are to issue fine porcelain collector plates featuring the Führer and other National Socialist Party big-hitters in honour of this occasion? Full marks to you!

I am very keen to receive advance details of this offer and if the edition is to be limited then I would certainly want to secure the earliest numbers possible. I am sending no money now.

Thanking you in advance.

Ihm fehlt einer!

Yours faithfully,

Ralph Tritt

THE BRADFORD GROUP
1 Castle Yard • Richmond • Surrey TW10 6TF
Telephone: 020 8939 9988 • Fax: 020 8332 6145 • E-Mail: customers@brad-ex.co.uk

6th June, 2000

Mr R Tritt
16 Sinclair Gardens
LONDON
W14 0AT

YOUR ACCOUNT NUMBER IS NONE FOUND
PLEASE QUOTE IT ON ALL CORRESPONDENCE

Dear Mr Tritt,

Thank you for your recent enquiry concerning the product *"Third Reich Fifty-Fifth Anniversary 1945 - 2000."*

Although The Bradford Group does produce a wide variety of product themes and titles, the above does not feature in any of our collections.

We are therefore sorry that we cannot provide you with any further information concerning the original supplier.

We are sorry that we cannot assist you at the present time, but thank you for your interest in our collections.

Yours sincerely,

**CLIENT SERVICES DEPARTMENT
THE BRADFORD GROUP**

World leaders in quality collectables

Offices in: Amsterdam • Auckland • Chicago • Frankfurt • London • London (Canada) • Milan • Paris • Stockholm • Sydney • Vienna • Zurich

TRITT COMESTIBLES

"No Nonsense Catering"

16 Sinclair Gardens, West Kensington, London W14 0AT

Friskies Petcare,
P.O. Box 53,
Newmarket,
Suffolk
CB8 8QF

9th September, 2000

Dear Sir/Madam,

I wonder, as a matter of interest, what is the likelihood of your Winalot products being a source of variant CJD? I ask specifically with regard to the duck and rabbit flavour.

Although these are not animals that have been linked with BSE, I notice that they constitute only 8% of the meat derivatives in this product, leaving something of a question mark over what makes up the rest. My concern is that offal from other types of animal with subclinical prion infection is also being used. If this is the case, am I right in thinking that the risk of contamination is lessened significantly when the product is boiled?

I would appreciate your setting my mind to rest on this.

Yours faithfully,

Ralph Tritt
MANAGING DIRECTOR

TRITT COMESTIBLES

"No Nonsense Catering"

16 Sinclair Gardens, West Kensington, London W14 0AT

Friskies Petcare,
P.O. Box 53,
Newmarket,
Suffolk
CB8 8QF

2nd October, 2000

Dear Sir/Madam,

I am enclosing a copy of a letter that I sent to you some weeks ago and to which I have had no reply.

I know that there have been problems with the postal service of late and that this is in no way a reflection of your own disorganization.

I would ask that you respond now as a matter of the gravest urgency.

Yours sincerely,

Ralph Tritt
MANAGING DIRECTOR

Encl.

MR RALPH TRITT
16 SINCLAIR GARDENS
LONDON
W14 0AT

04/10/00

Our Reference: 10057356/440572

Dear Mr Tritt

Thank you for contacting us regarding the meat derivatives that are used in Winalot Chunks In jelly. We apologise for the delay in replying to your letter.

As a matter of course, the Pet Food Manufacturers' Association, of which Friskies Petcare is a leading member, _only_ use raw material from animals which have been inspected and passed fit for human consumption. This certainly rules out the use of "dead on arrival" birds and poultry meat inspection rejects. In addition, PFMA members, including Friskies Petcare, have in place extensive and stringent quality control procedures of their own, which include audits with our suppliers.

We can assure you that all our suppliers know that such rules must be abided by.

The other ingredients in the food are made up of the moisture content, cereals, vegetables and minerals.

We hope this information has clarified the situation and may we thank you for allowing us the opportunity to reassure you on this matter.

If we can be of further assistance please do not hesitate to contact us again on our above freephone number.

Yours sincerely

Gayle Hammond
Pet Care Advisor

skies Pet Care, P.O. Box 53, Newmarket, Suffolk CB8 8QF
Tel: 0800 21 21 61 Fax: 01638 751 324
J.K.) Ltd. Registered in England No.121700. Registered Office: St. George's House, Croydon, Surrey, CR9 1NR

16 Sinclair Gardens,
London
W14 0AT

Gillette,
Customer Services Department,
London
TW7 5NP

18th September, 2000

Dear Sir/Madam,

I have recently switched to your Mach 3 shaving system and feel compelled to write in praise of the improved performance it gives. I've certainly never had it so close before wet and with so few strokes.

The future of shaving clearly lies in multi-bladed razors, but am I right in thinking that the Mach 3 is merely the thin end of the wedge? I understand that as early as 2010 we can expect to be using up to six blades at a time as a matter of course, making it possible to shave your entire face in a single stroke. Hopefully I'll be around long enough to see that day! It all seems quite incredible now when I look back all those years to when I first started shaving with a cut-throat.

Anyway, congratulations on a fine labour-saving product.

Yours faithfully,

Ralph Tritt

**Gillette
Group UK
Limited**

Gillette Consumer Services
PO Box 21, Aylesbury Road
Thame
Oxon, OX9 3LJ

Gillette - Shaving   0800 174543
Gillette - Toiletries   0800 374685
Duracell/Oral-B   0800 716434

Our Reference: 1886227A

22 September 2000

Mr R Tritt
16 Sinclair Gardens
London
W14 0AT

Dear Mr Tritt

Thank you for your letter from which I am delighted to learn of your successful use of the MACH3 Cartridges. You may be interested to learn that we have received more letters of praise for this product than any others we have launched.

May I thank you for taking the time and trouble to write to us with your comments.

Once again, many thanks.

If you have any questions, please do not hesitate to contact me on FREEPHONE 0800 174543.

Yours Sincerely,

Zoe. Eele

Zoe Eele
Consumer Relations Department

Enclosure:

A Subsidiary of The Gillette Company Registered office. Gillette Corner, Great West Road, Isleworth, Middlesex, TW7 5NP
Registered in England Under Registration No. 265048

16 Sinclair Gardens,
London
W14 0AT

Pedigree Masterfoods,
Freepost,
Melton Mowbray,
Leics.
LE13 0BR

16th October, 2000

Dear Sir/Madam,

My wife and I were obliged earlier this year to have our two year old mastiff, Van Outen, destroyed after he developed what can only be described as psychological problems.

Whilst he was alive, we fed the dog exclusively on Pedigree Chum with beef, and I am wondering now whether this would have had anything to do with his decline. You hear so much in the news today about CJD and BSE, but could this also affect pets as well as humans and cows? The dog didn't stagger or fall about as such, but he did have terrible mood swings and would suddenly snap without warning.

Don't get me wrong, I am not about to make any accusations or requests for compensation. (In any case, it's a bit late now for a post mortem as the dog ended up in the river.) I just wanted to know as a point of interest whether there is a risk of contamination from your products. Obviously the dogs aren't to know what they are eating, so what is there to stop you from using offal and ground up spinal cord in your recipe? Is this what you mean by "animal derivatives" as it says on the tin?

I doubt if John Gummer would have been so brave and sure of his position had he had to have eaten a bowl full of Pedigree Chum!

Yours faithfully,

Ralph Tritt

Pedigree Masterfoods
A Division of Mars U.K. Limited

By Appointment to
Her Majesty The Queen
Manufacturer of Canned Dog Food

Mr Ralph Tritt
16 Sinclair Gardens
London
W14 0AT

Dear Mr Tritt

19 Ocober 2000

Thank you for your letter.

We are sorry to hear that your Mastiff, Van Outen, was put to sleep earlier this year. It must have been a very distressing time for you both, and we understand why you may have questions that you would like answered. We will do our best to answer your letter as fully as possible.

Pedigree Masterfoods operate a rigorous selection and quality control procedure for all our meat purchasing and only use raw materials from healthy animals which have been inspected and declared fit for human consumption.

As you will appreciate in a highly competitive industry we are unable to divulge exact product recipes. The wording `animal derivatives' covers the fleshy parts of the animal carcass, these materials are those parts of the carcase not utilised or in excess of requirements for human food (for example lung, heart, liver, kidney and fish) but are still extremely nutritious for pet animals.

I have enclosed a statement which you may find useful. I hope you have found comfort with this reply. I'm sure Van Outen meant a great deal to you, and that you must miss him dearly.

If we can be of further help, please do not hesitate to contact the Technical Helpline at the number below.

Yours sincerely

Miss E Downing V N
Technical Communications

National Office, Waltham-on-the-Wolds, Melton Mowbray, Leicestershire LE14 4RS
Registered at the Companies Registration Office, London, England. Registered Number: 636458. Registered Office: 3D Dundee Road, Slough, Berkshire, SL1 4LG

R HELP & ADVICE ☎ 0800 717800 Technical Helpline   Facsimile: 01664 415232
Email: wal.customer.care@eu.effem.com

54

16 Sinclair Gardens,
London
W14 0AT

Customer Service Department,
Vecta,
Safeway Stores,
6 Millington Road,
Hayes,
Middlesex
UB3 4AY

23rd October, 2000

Dear Sir/Madam,

I am a keen consumer of your toilet flush blocks but dismayed by the lack of variety in colour available.

Is blue and green really all that you can come up with? What about something from the other end of the spectrum, even if it's only pastel shades? We've just had our bathroom decorated Deco Red and find ourselves now in the unhappy position of not being able to co-ordinate the lavatory water. I know that there is always the option of using translucent blocks, but then the pan doesn't really look clean to my eyes and so defeats the whole purpose of the product.

I am sure that there are many others like me who must feel the same way, so come on Vecta! Let's have a bit more imagination from you and then we can all really make a splash in the bathroom!

Yours faithfully,

Ralph Tritt

Our Ref: 137170a

3rd November 2000

Safeway Stores plc
Customer Services
Beddow Way
Aylesford
Nr Maidstone
Kent
ME20 7AT
Telephone 01622 712000
Facsimile 01622 712160

Mr R Tritt
16 Sinclair Gardens
London
W14 0AT

Dear Mr Tritt

We were very interested to receive your suggestions for alternative colours for our toilet flush blocks, other than blue and green. Thank you very much.

We welcome all our customers' opinions and I have made sure that your thoughts have been passed on in full to our buying department for this product and they will take your comments into account when review the range in the near future.

Thanks once again for contacting us.

Yours sincerely

Miss J Ferris
Customer Services Department
Direct Line: 01622 712926

Registered Office: 6 Millington Road, Hayes, Middlesex UB3 4AY. Registered in England. Registered No 746956 Telex 934888 DX 55400 Hayes (Middx)4.

16 Sinclair Gardens,
London
W14 0AT

Rowse Honey Ltd.,
Wallingford,
Oxon
OX10 9DE

23rd October, 2000

Dear Sir/Madam,

I am a keen consumer of your honey products and wonder whether you could settle a dispute that I am having with my wife?

I say that organic honey comes from free range bees that are allowed to nest naturally in hives that they have made themselves, but she maintains that it comes from bees that have been fed on flowers grown in manure. Who is right?

I know that some companys like Gale's use intensive farming methods and actually milk their bees by squeezing them with tweezers. We are not Buddhists or anything like that, but believe that all living things should be treated with respect, no matter how small or insignificant they might seem.

Anyway, rest assured that we will be staying loyal to your brand and traditions.

Best wishes to you and all the little workers!

Yours faithfully,

Ralph and Frances Tritt

ROWSE HONEY LTD.

MORETON AVENUE, WALLINGFORD, OXFORDSHIRE, OX10 9DE
TEL: 01491 827400 FAX: 01491 827434 E-MAIL: rowse.honey@rowsehoney.co.uk
www.rowsehoney.co.uk

Mr Ralph Tritt
16 Sinclair Gardens
London
W14 0AT

31 October 2000

Ref: SAB/JAF/10-31lttr-J

Dear Ralph

Re: Rowse Organic Honey

Thank you for your recent letter enquiring about what makes honey 'organic'.

I enclose for interest a copy of the current Soil Association Standard for Organic Honey. One of the key points is that beehives must be located at least 4 miles away from conventionally farmed land, or any source of inorganic pollution. (Bees fly up to 3-4 miles from their hives).

It is not possible to produce organic honey in the UK in any commercial quantities. For this reason the major producing countries of Rowse Organic honeys are:- Argentine, Mexico, Australia, New Zealand and Turkey.

It is not therefore necessary for bees to make their own hives – the beekeeper has a great responsibility to ensure that the hives are correctly located and managed.

Manure is not a vital ingredient either! The main areas producing organic honey are large expanses of unspoilt natural vegetation.

I hope that this settles your argument. Please accept with our compliments a jar of Rowse Organic Clear Honey (from Argentine) and Rowse Organic New Zealand Clover honey. These are two of my favourite honeys.

Yours sincerely

Stuart Bailey
Managing Director

INVESTOR IN PEOPLE

DIRECTORS: R.M. ROWSE · S.A. BAILEY · B.H. BUTCHER · A.S. ROWSE · B.C. ROWSE · REG. OFFICE: WALLINGFORD, OXFORD · REG. NO. 1024018 U

6.5 HONEY PRODUCTION

6.501   Honey must be taken from bees that forage only in organically cultivated areas or areas of natural vegetation which are free of herbicides and pesticides, and which have been so for a minimum of two years.

WELFARE

6.502   Hive management and honey extraction methods should be aimed at preserving the colony and sustaining it. The colony must not be destroyed when the honey is harvested.

6.503   The foundation of the comb used in the production of comb honey must be made from organically produced beeswax.

6.504   Permitted

1)   Selective breeding may be practised.

6.505   Prohibited

1)   Artificial insemination.

DIET

6.506   Hives must not be placed within 4 miles of conventionally farmed land, private gardens or areas subject to inorganic pollution such as roadside verges and roadways.

6.507   Permitted

1)   Only organically produced honey and natural pollen supplements.

6.508   Prohibited

1)   Other materials used for feeding - the hive must be taken out of Organic production for a minimum period of 12 months and all honey residues must be removed from the hive before it is returned to the production of organically produced honey.

VETERINARY PRACTICE

6.509   Permitted

1)   Wing clipping of queens.

2)   Biotechnical methods, formic acid fumigation and lactic acid sprays are permitted to control Varroa mite - no withdrawal period necessary.

3)   Chemical medicinal treatments of the bees other than permitted in 6.5092 above, only when the health of the colony is threatened. After such treatment, the hive must be immediately taken out of Organic production for a minimum of 12 months and all honey residues must be removed from the hive before it is returned to the production of organically produced honey.

TRANSPORT AND PROCESSING

6.510   All bulk containers must comply with the Packaging (see section 9.6), Transport (see section 9.7) and Labelling (see section 7.6) Standards.

6.511   All processing must comply with the Standards for Processing Organic Honey (see section 10.3).

16 Sinclair Gardens,
London
W14 0AT

National Federation Of Women's Institutes,
104 New Kings Road,
London
SW6 4LY

17th November, 2000

Dear Madam,

Please send me one of your 2001 nude calendars at £4.99. I am enclosing a postal order to the value of £5 and a large SAE accordingly.

Am I right in thinking that there is also a more racy version doing the rounds whereby you get to see everything? If this is the case, perhaps you would be kind enough to forward the details and advise of any discount for large orders. I am thinking in terms of twenty or so as Christmas presents for former colleagues at London Underground.

Anyway, fair play to you old birds for getting your kit off. Keep up the good work!

All the best for 2001.

Yours faithfully,

Ralph Tritt

National Federation
of Women's Institutes
104 New Kings Road
London SW6 4LY

tel: 020 7371 9300
fax: 020 7736 3652
e-mail: hq@nfwi.org.uk
website: www.nfwi.org.uk

RECYCLED PAPER

with compliments

NORTH YORKSHIRE WEST FEDERATION

W.I. Office
Alma House
Low St. Agnesgate
RIPON, HG4 1NA

Tel. (01765) 606339

Charity Reg. No. 513934

WI office does not supply the
Rylstone Calendar. Enquiries for
Mail Order can be made on
01280 814120

However I have seen them for sale in
WH Smiths unless this is just
With Compliments in the north.

16 Sinclair Gardens,
London
W14 0AT

The Whopping Women's Centre,
Philchurch Place,
Pinchin Street,
London
E1

4th December, 2000

Dear Madam,

I am interested in buying about twenty of your 2001 nude calendars and wonder whether you could let me know what they cost and if there is a discount for bulk.

They are to be Christmas presents for former colleagues at London Underground. Do you think that you can get them out for me in time?

I presume that the funds raised will be for your own use, but if this is not the case then I would like to know which charity will be benefitting.

Thank you for your help.

Yours faithfully,

Ralph Tritt

16 Sinclair Gardens,
London
W14 0AT

The Whopping Women's Centre,
Philchurch Place,
Pinchin Street,
London
E1

14th December, 2000

Dear Madam,

I wrote recently with regard to your 2001 nude calendar but have heard nothing back.

I appreciate that this must be a busy time for you, but I was hoping to place a large order (twenty or so) as Christmas presents for former work colleagues at London Underground.

I have enclosed a postal order to the value of £5 (I understand that the calendars are £4.99 each) with an SAE and wonder whether you could send me a sample post haste with details of any discount for bulk purchases.

Yours faithfully,

Ralph Tritt

Philchurch Place
off Pinchin Street London E1 1PJ
Tel/Fax 020 7702 0036

16 Sinclair Gardens,
LONDON,
W14 0AT

18th December 00

Dear Mr. Tritt,

I am writing in connection to your letter regarding some '2001 nude calendars'. I am sorry to disappoint you by saying that you have got the wrong address and company.

We are a community organisation and do not do any such things as 'nude calendars'. I do not know where you got the idea that we do such things, but I would like to correct you on this matter.

I am sending you back the postal order of £5 that came with your recent letter.

I would appreciate that you do not contact us again on such matters as this.

Yours Sincerely,

Development Worker

Community Garden Project

- a project of the Wapping Women's Centre

16 Sinclair Gardens,
London
W14 0AT

Consumer Services Manager,
The Ryvita Company Limited,
Old Wareham Road,,
Poole,
Dorset
BH12 4QW

12th January, 2001

Dear Sir/Madam,

My wife Frances and I are both keen consumers of your product as a healthy alternative to bread and have been eating it together for more years than we care to remember. It's the sheer versatility of the snack that we love so much.

I noticed on the packaging that you now have an internet site called www.ryvita.com for more information. Unfortunately, my wife and I don't have the internet and are concerned that we might be missing out on important Ryvita developments. Do you have a news letter so that people like us can keep abreast? If so, is there a cost for postage?

I am also thinking about sending off for one of your Ryvita tins but am concerned about it fitting through the letter box.

Yours faithfully,

Ralph Tritt

The Ryvita Company Limited
Old Wareham Road, Poole, Dorset BH12 4QW
Telephone: (01202) 743090
Fax: (01202) 732125

Our Ref: 11867/BLK

Mr R Tritt
16 Sinclair Gardens
London
W14 0AT

15 January, 2001

Dear Mr Tritt

Thank you for your letter expressing your interest in The Ryvita Company.

In answer to your questions, firstly our latest product is Ryvita Currant Crunch of which I have enclosed a packet for you to try. With regards to the Ryvita Tin, it will not fit through a letter box, but if you are not present on day of delivery, the tin is left at your nearest Post Office for collection at your convenience.

Thank you for again for your interest in our company.

Yours sincerely

Carla Gran
CONSUMER SERVICES DEPARTMENT

16 Sinclair Gardens,
London
W14 0AT

Carla Gran,
Consumer Services Department,
The Ryvita Company Limited,
Old Wareham Road,,
Poole,
Dorset
BH12 4QW

22nd January, 2001

Dear Ms. Gran,

Just a few lines to say how tickled my wife and I were to get a complimentary box of Ryvita Currant Crunch through the post. It was very thoughtful of you to go to that trouble and it made our day.

I have to say that you are on to a definite winner with this product and they taste good enough to eat with nothing on. In fact, my wife and I ate the whole packet that same day. The extra fruit and fibre is a positive boon for the stool too, as we both found out later to our cost!

However, it does seem that I was right to be concerned about missing out on Ryvita news through not being on the internet. Here is an excellent product that we know nothing about and could have been enjoying all along. It just goes to show that there is more to this internet than just looking at a lot of filth, but I'm too old now to get to grips with it. Is the Currant Crunch here to stay or is it just to mark your 75th anniversary (well done!)? I haven't seen it in the shops yet or on the TV. You don't say whether there is a regular news letter. Will you be able to keep me updated on any further developments?

I will definitely be sending off for an anniversary storage tin for my wife's birthday, but that's not for a few months yet and I don't want her coming across it and spoiling the surprise. Thank you for your reassurance with regard to the Consignia, as they call it now, and for your kindness in general. I am sure that you must be a lovely girl and a credit to the company.

Yours faithfully,

Ralph Tritt

Certificate No. FM 27202

RYVITA

The Ryvita Company Limited
Old Wareham Road, Poole, Dorset BH12 4QW
Telephone: (01202) 743090
Fax: (01202) 732125

By appointment to Her Majesty Queen Elizabeth
Manufacturers of Crispbreads
The Ryvita Co. Ltd. Poole, Dorset.

Mr R Tritt
16 Sinclair Gardens
London
W14 0AT

Our Ref: 11867/BLK

23 January, 2001

Dear Mr Tritt

Thank you for letter and kind words, they were very much appreciated.

We were pleased to learn that you and your wife thoroughly enjoyed the complementary packet of Ryvita Currant Crunch. We are glad to inform you that the product is here to stay for the foreseeable future.

Unfortunately we do not have a regular newsletter supplying information on our latest products. However, your comments have been forwarded to the Marketing Department, who may sometime in the future contact you by post with developments and projects that may be undertaken by the Ryvita Company Ltd.

Thank you once again for your interest in our company.

Yours sincerely

Carla Gran
CONSUMER SERVICES DEPARTMENT

68

Registered Office: Weston Centre, Bowater House, 68 Knightsbridge, London SW1X 7LQ. Registered in England Number 245
Directors: GH Weston • Guy Weston • Garth Weston • Zoe Withers • Philippe

16 Sinclair Gardens,
London
W14 0AT

Cadbury Ltd.,
P.O. Box 7011,
Bournville,
Birmingham
B30 2PY

3rd March, 2001

Dear Sir/Madam,

Seeing your Creme Eggs everywhere has reminded me that I wrote to you some weeks ago with regard to how my mother-in-law eats hers but have heard nothing back.

She's obliged, through illness, to poke them up her fundament and then absorb them through the wall of her bowel. Unconventional I know, and hardly suitable for one of your advertising campaigns, but surely worth an Easter voucher for the old girl?

The Creme Eggs are her favourite confectionery and provide what little succour she can glean in her twilight years.

Yours faithfully,

Ralph Tritt

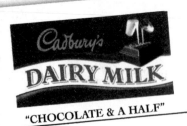

"CHOCOLATE & A HALF"

CADBURY LTD.

PO BOX 12
BOURNVILLE
BIRMINGHAM B30 2LU
CONSUMER DIRECT LINE 0121-451 4444
SWITCHBOARD TELEPHONE 0121-458 2000
FAX No. 0121-451 4297
http://www.cadbury.co.uk

April 6, 2001

Mr R Tritt
16 Sinclair Gardens
LONDON
W14 OAT

Our Ref:- 0730799A HFF

Dear Mr Tritt,

Thank you for your recent letter enquiring about publicity material.

All Cadbury publicity material is kept at a specialist, independent, handling house for distribution directly to the retail trade. We do not unfortunately hold stocks at Head Office for general distribution.

I am very sorry that we have been unable to help with your specific request. However, I am enclosing some fact cards on various aspects which I hope you will find of interest. I also return your postal order.

Yours sincerely

Helen Franklin
Consumer Relations Department

16 Sinclair Gardens,
London
W14 0AT

Burgerking UK,
Customer Services,
Charter Place,
Vine Street,
Uxbridge,
Middlesex
UB8 1BZ

13th March, 2001

Dear Sir/Madam,

First and foremost, my wife and I are both huge fans of your delicious food with a particular weakness for the Whopper meal. There is, however, one cause for concern that I would like to be reassured of with regard to this foot and mouth business.

I know that the disease is not supposed to affect humans, but they said the same thing about BSE in the beginning. It's just that my wife and I tend to eat your food every day and she has recently developed a rash between her toes (I'm all right so far). I've told her that it's probably nothing but she is too frightened to see the doctor. Is your beef from overseas and therefore safe? I'm sure that it is, but it would be good to set our minds at rest. If not, is it wise to be eating your stuff every day whilst this crisis is still on?

We were disappointed when the Shepherd's Bush branch of Burgerking closed down. My wife and I usually get the bus now to the ones in Earl's Court or Gloucester Road which makes for a good trip out. You just don't know what to believe on television these days, so I think we'll be sticking to the Chicken Royales until we hear back from you!

Yours faithfully,

Ralph Tritt

Ref # 158667

14 March, 2001

Mr Ralf Tritt
16 Sinclair Gardens
LONDON
W14 0AT

Dear Mr Tritt,

Thank you for your letter dated 13th March.

Firstly, we are pleased to read that you and your wife are big fans of Burger King.

Regarding Foot and Mouth disease, Burger King's primary concern is always for the safety and well being of its customers and we use only the finest quality ingredients, prepared to the highest standards of safety and hygiene. The current Foot and Mouth disease outbreak, although a setback for those in the British Meat industry, poses no threat to humans.

The beef we use in the UK comes from reputable, reliable European Sources with whom we have done business for several years.

All meat used Burger King is subject to a comprehensive range of quality checks before, after and during processing. This includes confirmed veterinary supervision at all stages. Burger King's suppliers all meet European Union standards to achieve maximum food safety.

With regards to the closure of the Shepherds Bush branch, please be assured that I will forward your comments to the relevant personnel.

I hope this answers your questions. Please do not hesitate to contact us again if you require any further information.

Yours sincerely,

Michael Plummer
Careline Co-Ordinator

BURGER KING (UK & EIRE)
Charter Place • Vine Street • Uxbridge, Middlesex UB8 1BZ
Careline: 08457 287437 (Local Charge: UK Mainland) • 1800 409 200 (Freephone: Eire) • Fax: 01895 206086
BurgerKing Limited. Registered Office: Edinburgh Park, 5 Lochside Way, Edinburgh, EH12 9DT. Registered No. 31456

A Diageo Company

72

16 Sinclair Gardens,
London
W14 0AT

Michael Plummer,
Careline Co-ordinator,
Burger King UK,
Charter Place,
Vine Street,
Uxbridge,
Middlesex
UB8 1BZ

19th March, 2001

Dear Mr. Plummer,

Thank you for your prompt reply and reassurance with regard to this foot and mouth business. You will no doubt be pleased to hear that my wife and I are back on the Whoppers!

It has occurred to me that there are probably quite a few other older folk out there who are unsure about what is fit to eat during this outbreak. Perhaps you'd do well to advertise what you said to me in your letter a bit more widely, even if it just meant having some signs put up in the window? It is a terrible thing to see all that meat going up in smoke when there is nothing wrong with it. Particularly when that's exactly what you'd be doing to it at Burger King anyway.

I have at last convinced my wife to see the doctor as the rash I mentioned has spread to other parts (round the teats). He says it may well be diet related and is also testing for allergies. I just wonder, is it good for her to be eating your stuff every day even if it is foot and mouth free? We do tend to eat the same meal, but would it be better balanced for her to mix and match a bit or is it really all the same?

Thank you for your help.

Yours sincerely,

Ralph Tritt

73

16 Sinclair Gardens,
London
W14 0AT

The Development Manager,
Vodafone Ltd.,
The Courtyard,
2-4 London Road,
Newbury,
Berkshire
RG14 1JX

19th March, 2001

Dear Sir/Madam,

I received one of your devices for Christmas from my wife and I have to say that, despite my reservations, I am beginning to warm to the thing!

I find the mobile particularly handy for confirming my location with my wife (in the supermarket, etc) but the concern still remains with regard to tumours in the head being caused through over use. I understand that this risk can be lessened with an ear-piece (not that I'd want to be bothered wearing one of those), although there are some who say that this is not the case at all and that they are in fact more dangerous still.

Anyway, the point to all this is that I have an idea that could be to everyone's benefit. Why not have a "conference" function on the mobile like so many telephones do in the office? This would enable the user to have two way conversations in perfect safety, with the mobile kept well away from his or her head, held perhaps with a clip to a lapel or inside pocket. Also, what a boon this would be on a train (my line of work, as it happens, until early retirement last year) allowing both hands to be kept free for other tasks.

I hope that this is food for thought for you boffins at Vodafone! Perhaps you have something similar lined up on the blackboard already, I don't know? It amazes me how quickly technology seems to change these days, we've a job out here trying to keep up with it all!

Yours faithfully,

Ralph Tritt

22nd March 2001

Ref: 122662248
Vodafone: Not Stated

Mr Ralph Tritt
16 Sinclair Gardens
London
W14 0AT

Dear Mr Tritt

Thank you for your recent letter regarding your Vodafone Mobile phone.

I appreciate your concerns about the health issues that have recently been raised with regards to using mobile phones. Vodafone continues to support scientific research and will keep everyone informed of any new developments.

If you would like further information regarding this matter, please contact the Department of Health website: www.doh.gov.uk/mobile.htm or write to the NRPB (National Radiological Protection Board) Chilton, Didcot, OX11 0RQ.

Vodafone are always grateful when receiving feedback from our customers, thank you for taking the time to forward your suggestions onto us as Vodafone.

Vodafone do not manufacture handsets, we provide them with a network. If you have any suggestions regarding the functions available on handsets you would need to forward them to the handset manufacturers.

If we can be of any further assistance, please do not hesitate to contact us on 191 from your Vodafone or 08700 776655 from a landline.

Yours sincerely

Debbie Bullivant
Customer Resolutions

Vodafone Central Services Limited

Pay as you Talk
1 Brindleyplace, Birmingham, B1 2JB

Registered Office. The Courtyard, 2-4 London Road, Newbury, Berkshire, England. Registered in England No. 3750974

75

16 Sinclair Gardens,
London
W14 0AT

Mr. Kipling Cakes,
Leigh Road,
Eastleigh,
Hants
SO50 9YY

20th April, 2001

Dear Sir/Madam,

My wife and I are both keen consumers of your extremely good cakes. We must have eaten our way through most of what you have to offer over the years but there is one old favourite I have yet to come across. I wonder, does Mr. Kipling have a cream horn in his repertoire?

Is there a list of cakes that you could send out? It would be fun to cross off the ones we've tried and also ear-mark those we haven't, like the horn. (If you do one, that is!)

Finally, is it true that Mr. Kipling is really in a home and that's why you never see his face in the adverts? I know that he must be very old by now and probably doesn't have much of an idea about what's going on with his business, but what a wonderful legacy he has left us.

Please send him my best regards, if that is possible.

Yours faithfully,

Ralph Tritt

Ref: 20719

02 May 2001

Mr Ralph Tritt
16 Sinclair Gardens
LONDON
W14 0AT

Dear Mr Tritt

Re: Mr Kipling Cakes

We were delighted to receive your complimentary letter. We are pleased to learn how much our customers enjoy our products and any suggestions.

At present we do not manufacture a cream horn, however we have passed a copy of your letter onto our Marketing Department for future consideration.

With regard to Mr Kipling himself, he is like Santa Claus in that a lot of mystery surrounds his existence. According to a recent poll almost a quarter of the population thought he did exist, which proves that Mr Kipling does indeed exist in the hearts and minds of our consumers, therefore we have passed your regards on to him!

Enclosed is a dietary sheet which lists all of our products we manufacture as requested.

We appreciate the interest you have shown in our affairs. Please accept the enclosed voucher as a gesture of our customer goodwill.

Yours sincerely

Mary Wright
Customer Care Administrator

Enc: £2.00 voucher

Manor Bakeries Limited, Leigh Road, Eastleigh, Hants. SO50 9YY, United Kingdom.
Telephone 023 8062 9966 Facsimile 023 8061 2041 www.mrkipling.co.uk
A company within the Rank Hovis McDougall Group. Registered in England number 289632. Registered office: Chapel Haute, Luton Road, Marlow, Bucks SL7 1LJ.
Mr Kipling is a Registered Trademark.

16 Sinclair Gardens,
London
W14 0AT

Customer Services,
Pizza Hut,
32 Goldsmith Road,
Woking,
Surrey
GU21 1JT

14th January, 2002

Dear Sir/Madam,

I get a lot of your leaflets through my door but I've never been a great one for foreign food. I'm a retired man and I like to know what I'm eating.

This, however, has set me thinking and I've come up with the idea for a Full English Pizza. Eggs, bacon, sausage, mushrooms and beans on a bread base with ketchup and cheese dressing. There's no reason either why you couldn't do a Sunday Roast Pizza, using Yorksire pudding instead of bread.

I think that these recipes would certainly be a winner with the older folk and probably prove popular with tourists as well.

Yours sincerely,

Ralph Tritt

Pizza Hut

Pizza Hut (UK) Limited
Customer Care Centre
One, Imperial Place
Elstree Way, Borehamwood
Hertfordshire WD6 IJN
Tel: 020-8732 9384
Fax: 020-8732 9009
Website: www.pizzahut.co.uk

Your reference is 0063955A

Mr Ralph Tritt
16 Sinclair Gardens
LONDON
W14 0AT

28 January 2002

Dear Mr Tritt,

Thank you for your letter regarding recipe suggestions.

I have today passed your comments to our Marketing Team for their information.

Assuring you of our best attention at all times.

Yours sincerely

Pippa Mordy
Customer Care Centre

CC: Marketing Team

Registered in England: 1072921

COMMERCIAL TRITT

THREE

16 Sinclair Gardens,
London
W14 0AT

The Commissioning Editor,
Hodder And Stoughton,
338 Euston Road,
London
NW1 3BH

7th February, 2000

Dear Sir/Madam,

I have just taken early retirement after thirty years in ticket supervision with London Underground. With time on my hands now and a recently purchased word processor I am keen to have a stab at writing about my experiences. It wouldn't just be memoirs as such but would also include funny incidents as well as a history of the Underground network and technical information. I would also cover customer care with tips on procedures and how to deal with the general public in various situations, reveal some of the tricks of the trade on how to make a few quid and expose some of the cover-ups and dodgy goings-on that I know for a fact.

I thought it would be a good idea to test the water first by writing to a few book people like yourself before actually starting the project. I feel that all those years spent in the job should amount to something and that people would enjoy reading about the experiences of an ordinary chap like myself. I think also that there is a huge interest in the Underground generally with up to 2.5 million people using it daily. The working title of the book is The Complete Tritt, which I think just about sums it up.

I am keen to hear your comments and feel sure that you will agree that this is definitely a runner (we can talk money later). I haven't written to any other publishers yet as I have always liked Hodder And Stoughton and wanted to give you first choice. But if you are up for it I might try and bring in the Evening Standard too with a sponsorship deal that could add to the takings considerably.

Yours faithfully,

Ralph Tritt

Hodder & Stoughton *Publishers*

TELEPHONE: 020 7873 6000
FAX: 020 7873 6024

16th February 2000

Mr. R. Tritt,
16 Sinclair Gardens,
London,
W14 OAT

Dear Mr. Tritt,

The Complete Tritt

Thank you for your letter of 7th February and for giving Hodder the chance to consider your proposal.

I'm afraid this doesn't seem right for our list so sadly we won't be able to make an offer of publication on this occasion. Hodder & Stoughton specialises in commercial fiction and non-fiction that is tailor-made for the mass-market and therefore we have to be confident of substantial sales quantities before taking a project on. Have you thought about writing your experiences, anecdotes and the history of the Underground, perhaps in a series, for the free paper Metro?

I'm sorry to disappoint you but you may want to try to find a literary agent and this you can do through the WRITERS' & ARTISTS' YEARBOOK or THE WRITERS' HANDBOOK.

We wish you better luck elsewhere.

Yours sincerely,

Betty Schwartz
Submissions Editor

HODDER & STOUGHTON LTD.
REGISTERED OFFICE:
338 EUSTON ROAD
LONDON NW1 3BH
COMPANY NO: 651692 ENGLAND
www.hodder.co.uk
A MEMBER OF THE HODDER HEADLINE PLC GROUP

16 Sinclair Gardens,
London
W14 0AT

The Artistic Director,
The Tate Gallery,
Millbank,
London
SW1

10th February, 2000

Dear Sir/Madam,

I have recently taken early retirement after 30 years in ticket supervision with London Underground and am looking for ways to keep busy and earn a bit of cash at the same time. A trip to your gallery last year has just prompted a bright idea that might be of some interest to you.

I remember seeing what I believe you call an installation of a chemist's by the vivisection man Damon Hurst which really is just a shopfitting. I won't pretend to understand it because I am not an artist, but I do know it is something that anyone could do. My idea would be to recreate the inside of a London Underground ticket office (the one at Earl's Court would be the right sort of size). I've worked in most of them over the years and have easy access to detailed plans.

If you think this is a good idea could you let me know which station you'd prefer so I can measure up. Also, would you expect me to build it myself or could we just get contractors in? I'd prefer contractors to be honest (as long as I got all the credit of course!) as I don't really have the tools. I'd want to call it something like Tritt's Utopia. And how does the money work? Would you buy it off me or would we wait for an independent buyer and split the proceeds? How much would it be worth for that matter? I haven't a clue.

I look forward to hearing from you.

Yours faithfully,

Ralph Tritt

16 Sinclair Gardens,
London
W14 0AT

The Artistic Director,
The Tate Gallery,
Millbank,
London
SW1

29th February, 2000

Dear Sir/Madam,   Reference Tritt's Utopia

I wrote to you some weeks ago with a proposal for an installation in one of the rooms of your gallery based on the interior of a London Underground ticket office but have heard nothing back.

I know you must be busy but surely there are people in your employ who can deal with these things? I am a busy man myself since taking early retirement and have a number of other projects on the go apart from this one so need to know where we stand as a matter of urgency.

If you are interested and have an available space we are looking at rough measurements of 10´ x 8´ x 12´. I am hoping to have the Evening Standard on board with a sponsorship deal and there is also the possibility of an accompanying book, working title The Complete Tritt.

Yours faithfully,

Ralph Tritt

Tate Gallery
Millbank
London
SW1P 4RG
Tel: 0171-887 8000
Fax: 0171-887 8007
Web: www.tate.org.uk

The National Collections of
British and Modern Art in
London, Liverpool and St Ives

TateGallery

8 March 2000

Ralph Tritt
16 Sinclair Gardens
London
W14 0AT

Dear Mr. Tritt,

Thank you for your letters dated 10 and 29 February, and for your proposal for an installation at the Tate. Please accept my apologies for not responding to you sooner.

I have discussed your proposal with a number of my colleagues. Whilst we appreciate your interest in the Tate and your imaginative suggestion, unfortunately we do not feel that this is appropriate.

I am sorry that we cannot be of assistance and wish you every success for the future, both with this and other projects.

Yours sincerely

Tim Batchelor
Programme Assistant

16 Sinclair Gardens,
London
W14 0AT

The Head Of Marketing,
The Evening Standard,
Northcliffe House,
London
W8 5TT

29th February, 2000

Dear Sir/Madam,

I have recently taken early retirement after thirty years in ticket supervision with London Underground and am looking for ways to keep busy and, at the same time, earn a bit of cash to supplement the pension. I have a couple of projects in the offing that might be of some interest to you.

First off, I am in negotiation with the Tate Gallery with regard to an installation as they like to call them of a London Underground ticket office (you might well have seen the one they have already of a chemist's by Damon Hurst). The piece to be entitled Tritt's Utopia. Secondly, I'm in negotiation also with publishers for an accompanying book based on my experiences with London Underground, working title The Complete Tritt.

It has occurred to me that with the association of your newspaper and the Underground being so strong, these projects could provide an ideal marketing opportunity for you if you were to chuck a bit of cash my way in return for some sort of sponsorship deal. I will have to check on the commercial ramifications with the Tate, but the publisher looks like being Faber & Faber and I'm sure they will be up for it.

It's early days yet, but I'm hoping to get things moving very quickly on this and would appreciate a prompt reply if you want to be a part of it.

Yours faithfully,

Ralph Tritt

Daily Mail and General Holdings Limited

Northcliffe House, 2 Derry Street, London W8 5TT Telephone: 020-7938 6682 Fax: 020-7938 4890
E-mail: vyvyan.harmsworth@dmgt.co.uk

V.P.W. Harmsworth, LVO
Director of Corporate Affairs

Mr Ralph Tritt
16 Sinclair Gardens
London W14 0AT

3rd March 2000

Dear Mr Tritt,

Thank you for your letter of 29th February. I have forwarded it to the editor of Metro newspaper which, as you will know, has a strong Underground connection.

If they wish to follow up your suggestions they will be in touch with you direct.

16 Sinclair Gardens,
London
W14 0AT

The Chief Handler,
Battersea Dogs Home,
Battersea Bridge Road,
London
SW11

12th March, 2000

Dear Sir/Madam,

I wonder if you could be of service to me with an artistic project I have planned at the Tate Gallery?

I am negotiating with a chap called Tim Batchelor regarding a piece to be entitled Dogsbodies that will consist of a nest of bisected dog carcasses set in a formaldehyde filled tank. My problem at the moment is in the supply of raw materials and this is where I hope you will be able to come in.

I am aiming to have at least four different breeds in the tank, starting with something fairly big like a Saint Bernard and ending maybe with one of those little snapping lap dogs like a pug. I would be open to suggestions here on a more precise selection and would obviously prefer the dogs dead on delivery. I already have the help of a professional butcher with regard to the assemblage.

I hope you can help with this as I know you must have more dogs than you can cope with and a lot of them will have to be put down anyway. To be honest I don't know who else to contact. Veterinarians seem unwilling to co-operate and I don't want to get into trouble with the RSPCA by going to a pet shop and dispatching the things myself. I would be happy to make a financial contribution to your organization and could even give you a plug in the catalogue.

This is a formal approach. If you are amenable to the idea then perhaps I could give you a ring or we could meet up to discuss things further?

Yours faithfully,

Ralph Tritt

Battersea Dogs Home
Patron: Her Majesty The Queen
President: His Royal Highness Prince Michael of Ker

4 Battersea Park Road, London SW8 4A
Tel: 020-7622 3626   Fax: 020-7622 64
www.dogshome.org

Ralph Tritt
16 Sinclair Gardens
LONDON
W14 0AT

14th March 2000

Dear Mr Tritt

We are in receipt of your letter dated 12th March.

Battersea Dogs Home has no intention whatsoever to be involved in the project that you describe. We are an animal rescue organisation and are frankly horrified by your proposals. I gather from the Tate Gallery that they are also unwilling to be involved.

Yours sincerely

Carol Heatly
Manager

Battersea Dogs Home
4 Battersea Park Road,
London SW8 4AA
Tel: 020-7622 3626
Fax: 020-7622 6451

Battersea at Bell Mead
Priest Hill, Old Windsor,
Berkshire SL4 2JN
Tel: 01784 432929
Fax: 01784 471538

Battersea at Brands Hatch
Crowhurst Lane, Ash,
Kent TN15 7HH
Tel: 01474 874994
Fax: 01474 872855

A Member of The Association of British Dogs and Cats Homes
Company Limited by Guarantee, Registered in England No. 278802   Registered as a Charity under the Charities Act 1960 No. 206394
Registered Office: The Dogs Home Battersea, 4 Battersea Park Road, London, SW8 4AA

TO/BD2 12/99

Mr Ralph Tritt
16 Sinclair Gardens
London
W14 0AT

13th March 2000

Ref:13-03-01

Dear Mr Tritt,

Your letter regarding your planned book has been passed on to me and it certainly does sound interesting.

I have taken the liberty of forwarding your letter on to the organisers of the Metro Travel Page, who regularly do features on the underground.

Yours sincerely,

Ian MacGregor
EDITOR

Harmsworth Quays Printing, Surrey Quays Road, Rotherhithe, London SE16 1PJ TEL: 0171 651 5200 FAX: 0171 651 5202

London Metro is a trading name of Associated London Metro Limited, part of the Associated Newspapers Group. Registered in England No. 3635489. Registered Office. Northcliffe House, 2 Derry Street, Kensington, London W8 5TT

16 Sinclair Gardens,
London
W14 0AT

Tim Batchelor,
Programme Assistant,
The Tate Gallery,
Millbank,
London
SW1

13th March, 2000

Dear Mr. Batchelor,

Thank you for your recent letter declining my idea for an installation at the gallery. It is a pity because I'm on the verge of getting Metro the free London Underground newspaper on board as sponsor. Never mind. At least my book is still a runner.

I've since been struck with another idea while watching Crufts 2000 and thought it worth giving you first refusal as, once again, it's pretty much in your neck of the woods. I propose a nest of bisected dog carcasses set in a formaldehyde filled tank entitled Dogsbodies. I am lucky enough to have the professional services of my local butcher Perry Edgbaston at my disposal, and I've also approached Battersea Dogs Home regarding the supply of raw materials. I took the liberty of using your name at the gallery as reference to help speed things along.

I think it will prove impossible to find a sponsor for this one but I intend to continue anyway as I think it is such a strong idea. As I have said before, I am not a professional artist but this sort of thing is like meat and drink to me. Perhaps I could give you a ring at work to discuss this further on a more personal level and you could even pop over in a week or so to see the work in progress?

Best wishes,

Ralph Tritt

Tate Gallery
Millbank
London
SW1P 4RG
Tel: 0171-887 8000
Fax: 0171-887 8007
Web: www.tate.org.uk

TateGallery

15 March 2000

Ralph Tritt
16 Sinclair Gardens
London
W14 0AT

Dear Mr. Tritt,

Thank you for your letter dated 13 March. I'm afraid we must also decline your second proposal for an exhibition at the Tate. I would ask that you refrain from using my name or that of the Tate Gallery in your endeavours to realise this project as we wish no association with it.

Yours sincerely.

Tim Batchelor
Programme Assistant

TRITT Inc.

16 Sinclair Gardens, West Kensington, London W14 0AT

Lord Andrew Lloyd Webber,
Really Useful Group Ltd.,
22 Tower Street,
London
WC2H 9NS

18th May, 2000

Dear Lord Lloyd Webber,

Please forgive the temporary stationery but my itinerary is such that I can delay no longer.

I am planning to open off-west end in the autumn with my musical celebration of the London Underground entitled Wheels Of Steel: Rock And Rolling Stock. I am at present putting together a production team and expect the necessary funding to be in place by early June. I have a choice of venues pencilled and am about to begin casting but none of this need concern you.

Lyrically the work is all mine so that isn't an issue either. The score too, although I have taken as my inspiration certain classical pieces now back in the public domain. Debussy's Suite Bergamasque, for example, where Clair De Lune becomes Mind The Gap, and the intermezzo from Sibelius' Karelia Suite is now called Zones! (1, 2, 3, 4, 5 & 6). But again this needn't concern you. It is the staging that I am worried about as I intend the whole thing to be performed on roller skates much like your own Starlight Express.

I know of course that you do not hold the copyright to roller skating per se, but at the same time I am not prepared to run the risk of incurring your wrath and an expensive legal action to boot! Is this something that you would object to strongly or is there a way in which we can reach a happy compromise? You'll know how hard it is to get these sort of projects off the ground and I really am working on a shoestring budget. It would make all the difference if we could resolve this quickly and easily.

Yours sincerely,

Ralph Tritt
PRODUCER

TRITT Inc.

16 Sinclair Gardens, West Kensington, London W14 0AT

Lord Andrew Lloyd Webber,
Really Useful Group Ltd.,
22 Tower Street,
London
WC2H 9NS

2nd June, 2000

Dear Lord Lloyd Webber,

I wrote to you a few weeks ago with regard to my musical production Wheels Of Steel: Rock And Rolling Stock, set for an off-west end run in the autumn. If you recall, I shall be replicating your own staging from Starlight Express and, not being a litigious sort, was keen to garner your approval. I know that you are a very busy man and so I shall register your lack of response as a blessing to go ahead.

I have already been down to the Apollo Victoria on a number of occasions taking notes and so will not be requiring any complimentaries. I'm quite happy to pay my way in this respect as it's the least I can do! Rest assured, however, that you will be guest of honour at the opening of my own little diversion. I'll keep you posted!

Thank you once again for the gesture and my best regards to Mr. Stilgoe.

Yours sincerely,

Ralph Tritt
PRODUCER

THE REALLY USEFUL GROUP LIMITED

22 Tower Street, London WC2H 9NS
Tel: 020 7240 0880 Fax: 020 7240 1204 www.reallyuseful.com

3 July 2000

My Direct Fax No: 0171-539 8251

R Tritt
Tritt Inc.
16 Sinclair Gardens
West Kensington
London W14 0AT

Dear Mr Tritt

Wheels of Steel: Rock and Rolling Stock

Your letters dated 18 May and 2 June 2000 have been passed directly to me, without having been seen by the addressee, Lord Lloyd Webber.

As you will appreciate, Lord Lloyd Webber has an extremely busy schedule and is unable to reply personally to the many letters he receives. Of course, Lord Lloyd Webber's failure to respond to your unsolicited correspondence in no way constitutes deemed approval of your venture.

The Really Useful Group Limited is the worldwide owner of the copyright, music and lyrics of the dramatico-musical work, Starlight Express, together with the directions, choreography and designs of the London production.

A dramatic performance such as "Wheels of Steel: Rock and Rolling Stock" as described by you, which incorporates our copyright requires our permission. I regret to inform you that we do not grant our permission for your use of our copyright or any other intellectual property rights owned or controlled by us.

It is our firm policy to refuse to grant permission for such ventures, so that our intellectual property rights are protected. Our policy is to ensure that our intellectual property rights are only used to promote the products and services of The Really Useful Group Limited, its subsidiaries and affiliates.

I must reserve The Really Useful Group Limited's rights and remedies in respect of any unauthorised use of its intellectual property rights.

Yours sincerely

Emma Topping
Legal Affairs Assistant

cc: Jan Eade
Sam Burgess

TRITT Inc.

16 Sinclair Gardens, West Kensington, London W14 0AT

Ainsley Harriott,
Ainsley's Barbecue Bible,
BBC Television Centre,
Wood Lane,
London
W12 7RJ

19th May, 2000

Dear Mr. Herriott,

I am sorry to have to write to you care of the BBC but I have been unable to discover who represents you.

I am planning to open off-west end in the autumn with my own production of Wheels Of Steel: Rock And Rolling Stock, a musical celebration of the London Underground. I hope to have sufficient backing in place within the next few weeks (a combination of private investment and national lottery funding) and am just beginning to think about casting. Having already auditioned and engaged a chorus line of seasoned professionals, I am naturally keen to add a few celebrity faces (in perhaps unexpected roles) in order to give the production and, of course, the box office that little extra frisson. To this end I should like to offer you the part of Northern Line Station Master, Gospel Oak.

I am aware that you are a natural performer and can probably sing and dance a bit too, but the main requirement here will be a sense of balance as, with Lord Andrew Lloyd Webber's blessing, the production will be staged on roller skates á la Starlight Express. I have provisionally pencilled a limited six week run, but who knows what may happen after that?

If you think this is something you would like to be a part of, could you please in the first instance write back letting me know who your agent is? The sooner we can broach the business of fees and time-scale, etc the better.

I hope we can work together.

Yours sincerely,

Ralph Tritt
PRODUCER

JEREMY HICKS ASSOCIATES

12 OGLE STREET   LONDON W1P 7LG
Tel 0171 636 8008   Fax 0171 636 8880

30 May 2000

Ralph Tritt
TRITT INC.
16 Sinclair Gardens
London W14 0AT

Dear Mr. Trott

Many thanks for your letter to Ainsley Harriott, which has eventually found its way to us. We are his agents.

Your production, *Wheels Of Steel: Rock And Rolling Stock*, sounds fascinating and, in keeping with the subject matter, is long overdue. But before we ink in dates for rehearsals, costume fittings and promotional interviews, we do need to cover a few points (no pun).

Does Gospel Oak have a big part? I expect all your celebs ask that question, but Ainsley was wondering whether it might be possible for him to phone in his performance; that way you would get the authentic crackle of a station announcement while saving the cost of a pair of roller skates.

Who will be playing the part of Russell Square? It's on his way home and, if it's someone he knows, he might be able to get a lift.

How far off-West End do you intend to be? I suppose we could consider any postal district beginning with a W, but somewhere *really* off-West End - Sunderland, for instance - might be trickier.

As to fees and time-scale . . . well, his fees are high and his time-scale even higher, so it's clearly not a done deal. However, you never know. This could either be a runaway success or a signal failure.

Yours sincerely

Jeremy Hicks

Jeremy Hicks

TRITT Inc.

16 Sinclair Gardens, West Kensington, London W14 0AT

Sir Richard Branson,
Virgin Ltd.,
120 Campden Hill Road,
London
W8

21st May, 2000

Dear Sir Richard,

I am a small independent producer hoping to open off-west end in the autumn with my own production of Wheels Of Steel: Rock And Rolling Stock, a musical celebration of the London Underground. Although I expect to have sufficient backing in the shape of national lottery funding in place within the next few weeks, as a man after my own heart you will know the value of contingency. I am therefore taking this opportunity to write to patrons of the arts such as yourself with an invitation of private investment.

The score is an original pop reworking of classical favourites much in the style of Lord Andrew Lloyd Webber, and the staging, with the great man's blessing, will be similar to that of Starlight Express, i.e. on skates. The key to the production is the extraordinary casting of celebrities. Although it is still too early to confirm names, I can tell you that I have approached Bob Geldof for the role of itinerant narrator, Kilburn Park; Ainsley Harriott as Northern Line station master, Gospel Oak; Sian Lloyd as star-crossed lover Dollis Hill; Mariella Frostrup representing the Docklands Light Railway as Mudchute; and A. A. Gill as the affected and slightly sinister Theydon Bois. I am also hoping to secure top DJ Kid Jensen as Piccadilly Line pop-picker Boston Manor. I will not, of course, be leaving anything to chance with regard to the hoofing and vocal performances and have already assigned a troupe of seasoned professionals to take care of that. The celebrities will be on board primarily for their appeal at the box office.

I anticipate a provisional run of six weeks and, at this early stage, would be prepared to guarantee a 10% return on whatever you care to invest with increments based on the net box office to be agreed once the show hits profit.

Yours sincerely,

Ralph Tritt
PRODUCER

Virgin Enterprises Ltd

120 Campden Hill Road, London W8 7AR
Tel: 020-7313 2000 Fax: 020-7727 8200

Our Ref: dg/250500/si

25th May 2000

Mr R Tritt
Tritt Inc
16 Sinclair Gardens
West Kensington
London
W14 0AT

Dear Ralph

Many thanks for your letter.

Your idea certainly seems an interesting one, however, I am concentrating investment on ideas which fit in with my existing businesses at present. Your idea is a little too far removed from those businesses for me to become involved.

I wish you the best of luck.

Kind regards

Richard Branson
Chairman
Virgin Group of Companies

Dictated by Richard Branson and signed in his absence

Registered Office: 120 Campden Hill Road, London W8 7AR. Registered in England No. 1073929

TRITT Inc.

16 Sinclair Gardens, West Kensington, London W14 0AT

Mariella Frostrup,
News Of The World,
1 Virginia Street,
London
E1 9BD

20th May, 2000

Dear Ms. Frostrup,

I am sorry to have to write to you care of the newspaper but I have been unable to locate the name of your agent.

I am currently casting for my own production of Wheels Of Steel: Rock And Rolling Stock, a musical celebration of London Underground, and was wondering whether you would be interested in representing the Docklands Light Railway in the role of Mudchute? To be honest you are not my first choice, but having since approached Bob Geldof for the part of the narrator, Kilburn Park, it has been decided, under the circumstances, that Paula Yates' involvement would be inappropriate.

Please do not concern yourself at this point with having to sing and dance as I have already engaged a professional troupe to deal with that. Some ability to skate, however, would be to your advantage as the staging, with Lord Andrew Lloyd Webber's blessing, will be much the same as Starlight Express. There will not be any call for nudity.

I am anticipating a six week run off-west end to open in the autumn and should have the necessary funding in place within the next few weeks courtesy of the national lottery. If you feel as though you would like to be a part of this production, please put me in touch with your management at the earliest opportunity to talk money. I am thinking initially of a guarantee with a split after costs as I know you'll be good for our box office. We can discuss your part in more detail once this is out of the way.

I hope we can work together.

Yours sincerely,

Ralph Tritt
PRODUCER

BRAZEN HUSKY

7 June 2000

Ralph Tritt
Producer
Tritt Inc
16 Sinclair Gardens
West Kensington
London
W14 OAT

Dear Ralph

My agents number is ▮▮▮▮▮▮. Am currently practising my skating skills on Peru's Inca Trail. In my absence you could get in touch with Melanie Coupland on the above number.

All the best

Mariella Frostrup

TRITT Inc.

16 Sinclair Gardens, West Kensington, London W14 0AT

Jeremy Hicks,
Jeremy Hicks Associates,
12 Ogle Street,
London
W1P 7LG

9th June, 2000

Dear Mr. Hicks,

Thank you for your interest in my musical production, Wheels Of Steel: Rock And Rolling Stock.

It is with some regret that I must now inform you of its postponement due to overwhelming financial circumstances. The show's two main backers have withdrawn their support and there is some doubt as to whether I will be able to satisfy the criteria laid down by the Art's Council in order to qualify for small scale capital funding. In any case, their assessment will take up to four months thus prohibiting any chance of an autumn run.

Please extend my very best regards to your client, Ainsley Harriott, and I am sorry if he has been inconvenienced in any way. I should like to think that I could make another approach in the new year once this little aberration has been resolved. The show must go on!

Yours sincerely,

Ralph Tritt
PRODUCER

Dictated by Ralph Tritt and signed in his absence

TRITT COMESTIBLES

"No Nonsense Catering"

16 Sinclair Gardens, West Kensington, London W14 0AT

The Commercial Director,
Great Eastern Railway Ltd.,
35 Artillery Lane,
London
E1 7LP

9th September, 2000

Dear Sir,

As a former employee of London Underground, I am looking now to raise my sights and branch out into other areas of our great communications network with a second career. To this end, I wonder if you would be good enough to put me straight on a few points?

Are your buffet cars operated on a franchise basis or is the catering done "in-house"? Either way, as the director of a small but ambitious catering company, what are my chances of becoming involved or, at least, making a serious pitch for the business and how should I best go about it?

All too often today I notice the disaffection caused by what we are promised and expect to receive far exceeding the end result. This is as true of the catering industry as it is of any other, particular when food is being prepared under difficult circumstances such as on a railway. But why be overly ambitious and fail when you can do the simple things well? And because it's simple, you can always be consistent. I'm talking gammon ham and gala pie with lots of pickle. Quiche lorraine and croquette potatoes by all means for the more exotic tastes, but none of this nouvelle cuisine nonsense. What people want is proper portions of good, wholesome food, not pale imitations of Gordon Ramsay served up in a plastic box with a name they can't even pronounce. I believe there is a back-to-basics movement afoot and that we can all steal a march by responding to it now.

Anyway, this is not the time or the place to expound further but you get my point. I have a business plan and am about to start shooting a corporate video with TV chef Rustie Lee. I look forward to hearing back from you and to receiving contractual details as well as information on budgets, outlay, etc in due course. In the meantime, I'll be able to get a proper presentation together that will give you a better idea of what I am about.

Yours faithfully,

Ralph Tritt
MANAGING DIRECTOR

Great Eastern Railway Ltd
35 Artillery Lane
London
E1 7LP

To: Mr. Ralph Tritt
Managing Director,
Tritt Comestibles,
16 Sinclair Gardens,
West Kensington,
London,
W14 OAT.

First 🚄

From: Richard Clark

Date: 26th September 2000
Tele: 020-7904-3310

Dear Mr. Tritt,

I have been passed a copy of your letter to the Commercial Director of First Great Eastern.

As the Manager responsible for Catering/Retail provision on both stations and trains, I have been asked to respond. Unfortunately my Contract Manager is on Annual Leave until 2nd October. I have however, asked that he contact you on his return to discuss your requirements.

Yours sincerely,

RICHARD CLARK
RETAIL MANAGER

Registered Office
32A Weymouth Street, London W1N 3FA
Registered in England No 3007936

A **First**Group 🚄 Company

cpt
member

TRITT COMESTIBLES

"No Nonsense Catering"

16 Sinclair Gardens, West Kensington, London W14 0AT

The Marketing Director,
Tesco Stores Ltd.,
Cheshunt,
Herts
EN8 9SL

11th September, 2000

Dear Sir/Madam,

I am head of a small, independent catering company looking to capitalise on the increasing demand for horse meat.

As you will know, all of the meat reaching our tables at present comes from the continent, turning what should be a cheap alternative into something that is prohibitively expensive. It is my aim to cut costs in half by going for home produced stock and I am currently in negotiation with both Havana Horse (UK) Ltd. and Hyde Park Stables as potential suppliers.

I am wondering now whether Tesco will be considering entering this market and, if so, whether any of my new lines, already at the trial stage, would be of any interest to you for your own brand? Firstly, the Horse Bap And Rider© combination comprising steak in a bun with a choice of "rider" that includes cheese, bacon and pimento. Secondly, the slightly more upmarket Cheval De Feu©, prime slices of flame-grilled fillet. And lastly, for the kids, Hoofers©, bite-sized pieces of horse in a crispy batter with dipping sauce.

If you are at all interested in any of these lines, please reply at your earliest convenience as I will be approaching a number of other outlets. I would be delighted to stage a sampling either at your depot or in my own kitchens.

Yours faithfully,

Ralph Tritt
MANAGING DIRECTOR

Our Ref: 2153744

20 September 2000

Mr R Tritt
16 Sinclair Gardens
LONDON
W14 0AT

Customer Service
PO Box 73
Baird Avenue
Dundee
DD1 9NF
Freephone   0800 505555

Dear Mr Tritt

Thank you for your letter received on 20th September, with reference to you asking us to stock horse meat.

Our Buyers decide what our stores sell and I have asked our Buyer for this product range to consider your request. As we stock products according to their popularity and the amount of available space, I cannot say at this stage whether or not we will start selling this product.

Thank you for taking the time and trouble to write to us. We do like to hear from our customers. Your comments and suggestions help us to decide what products we sell and the policies we follow. I hope we may look forward to your continued and valued custom.

Yours sincerely
For and on behalf of Tesco Stores Ltd

Gillian Mcnally
Customer Service Manager

Stores Ltd. (519500). Company Registered in England. Registered Office: Tesco House, Delamare Road, Cheshunt, Waltham Cross, Hertfordshire. EN8 9SL.

TRITT COMESTIBLES

"No Nonsense Catering"

16 Sinclair Gardens, West Kensington, London W14 0AT

Gillian McNally,
Tesco Customer Services,
P.O. Box 73,
Baird Avenue,
Dundee
DD1 9NF

23rd September, 2000

Dear Ms. McNally,

I am in receipt of your letter dated 20th September and fear that you may have misunderstood my original proposal.

I do not want Tesco to stock horse meat that I might buy it for myself. To be perfectly frank with you, I have more of the stuff in my refrigerator than you could shake a stick at. What I am suggesting is that Tesco stock the lines I have originated and detail in my letter.

I trust that the letter is still on file and will be passed to your buyer for its contents to be considered. Please don't hesitate to contact me if you require a copy.

Yours sincerely,

Ralph Tritt
MANAGING DIRECTOR

Our Ref: 2173217

26 September 2000

Customer Service
PO Box 73
Baird Avenue
Dundee
DD1 9NF
Freephone   0800 505555

Mr R Tritt
16 Sinclair Gardens
LONDON
W14 0AT

Dear Mr Tritt

Thank you for your letter received on 26th September.

I was interested to read your further comments. I would like to assure you that I have carefully recorded your views and will pass them on, together with any others we may receive, for the consideration of the appropriate personnel.

Thank you for taking the time and trouble to contact us again on this issue.

Yours sincerely
For and on behalf of Tesco Stores Ltd

Gillian Mcnally
Customer Service Manager

o Stores Ltd. (519500). Company Registered in England. Registered Office: Tesco House, Delamare Road, Cheshunt, Waltham Cross, Hertfordshire. EN8 9SL.

TRITT COMESTIBLES
"No Nonsense Catering"
16 Sinclair Gardens, West Kensington, London W14 0AT

Personally Speaking,
2 Hartopp Road,
Four Oaks,
Sutton Coldfield,
West Midlands
B74 2RH

23rd September, 2000

Dear Sir/Madam,

I am about to make a pitch for a railway catering franchise and to this end require a corporate video as a matter of urgency. Would you be good enough to advise of a ballpark figure and approximately how long it would take to put such a thing together? I need to make a presentation in November.

I notice that you have a number of "foodies" on your roster but suspect that stars of the calibre of Antony Worrall Thompson and Michael Winner would be outside my budget. Rustie Lee, on the other hand, would seem ideal. I am sure that all of that unfortunate business with the shoplifting must have long since blown over, and I for one would have no qualms whatsover about engaging her providing such considerations were reflected in the fee. She is, after all, where Ainsley Harriott got his act from and deserves a second chance. Aside from all that, she would fit in perfectly with my back-to-basics approach.

Perhaps I can give you a ring once you've put me on track with all of this? You will obviously want to know more about my business plan and I would like to discuss the feasibility of a number of ideas that I think we can use.

I hope we can work together.

Yours faithfully,

Ralph Tritt
MANAGING DIRECTOR

The people for
corporate entertainment
excellence

26 September 2000

Mr Ralph Tritt
16 Sinclair Gardens
West Kensington
London
W14 0AT

Dear Mr Tritt

Re: Rustie Lee

I am in receipt of your letter dated 23 September 2000 regarding availability and costing for Rustie Lee. If you care to telephone me, I would like to discuss the matter further with you.

Yours sincerely

Norman Phillips
Managing Director

Phillips Organisation Ltd · Longridge House · 2 Hartopp Road · Sutton Coldfield · West Midlands · B74 2RH · Tel: 0121 308 1267
web: www.NormanPhillips.co.uk · E-mail: info@NormanPhillips.co.uk   Registered in England No.

TRITT COMESTIBLES

"No Nonsense Catering"

16 Sinclair Gardens, West Kensington, London W14 0AT

The Manager,
Havana Horse (UK) Ltd.,
20 Kinnerton Street,
London
SW1X

9th October, 2000

Dear Sir,

I have written a couple of times now with regard to the possible provision of animals under four years for the table but have heard nothing back.

To be honest, I am having a hard time trying to find a willing supplier and would greatly appreciate your co-operation in an advisory capacity if nothing else. I have already aroused interest at Tesco with a number of equine based snack ideas and am currently waiting to hear back from the Harvester restaurant group.

I look forward to hearing from you.

Yours faithfully,

Ralph Tritt
MANAGING DIRECTOR

HAVANA HORSE (U.K.) LTD

BLOODSTOCK AGENCY

20 KINNERTON STREET, LONDON SW1X 8ES, ENGLAND
TELEPHONE: 0171-235 5704   FACSIMILE: 0171-235 6389
TELEPHONE: 07000 HAVANA   E-MAIL: HAVHORSES@AOL.COM

Ralph Tritt
Tritt Comestibles
16 Sinclair Gardens
West Kensington
London
W14 0AT

19 October 2000

Dear Mr Tritt

Thank you very much for your letters of 23 September and 9 October.

Unfortunately I am unable to help you as we buy and sell live horses, not meat.

Yours sincerely

ANDY J SMITH

REGISTERED OFFICE: 416 WEST GREEN ROAD, LONDON N15 3PU
REGISTERED IN ENGLAND NO. 2995404   VAT REGISTRATION NO. 649 9857 55

Mr R Tritt
Managing Director
Tritt Comestibles
16 Sinclair Gardens
West Kensington
London
W14 0AT

Tel: 0207 904 3307
Fax: 0207 904 3313

03 October 2000

Dear Mr Tritt

Thank you for your recent letter that has been passed onto me. I understand that Richard Clark has written to you in my absence.

I see that you make reference in your letter to buffet cars, however First Great Eastern does not run any buffet cars on their services. We do operate a trolley service on certain train services Monday to Saturday provided by an outside contractor. This is an annual contract due for renewal in December this year.

Could you advise me if indeed you are purely seeking operation of buffet car facilities or is there interest in the provision of a trolley service. Our current contractor has been with us for two years and while I am happy with their operation I am always open to new ideas and opportunities.

I look forward to hearing from you.

Yours sincerely

Steve Whitehead
Retail Policy Manager

Registered Office
32A Weymouth Street, London W1N 3FA
Registered in England No 3007936

A FirstGroup 🍂 Company

TRITT COMESTIBLES

"No Nonsense Catering"

16 Sinclair Gardens, West Kensington, London W14 0AT

Steve Whitehead,
Retail Policy Manager,
Great Eastern Railway Ltd.,
35 Artillery Lane,
London
E1 7LP

12th October, 2000

Dear Mr. Whitehead,

Thank you for your recent letter with regard to the Great Eastern trolley service contract.

I have thought long and hard about the logistics of such a commitment were I to take it on and concluded, with regret, that it is not for me. The buffet car is really the only place I can see myself operating viably, with multiple covers and substantial meals being served, as opposed to just snacks and confectionery.

As for your being open to new ideas, I am quite sure that what you don't know about railway facilities you could write on the back of a return ticket to Wivenhoe. You won't want me stating the obvious, that much is certain. There is, however, one suggestion I have that you may want to consider. I am currently dealing in horse meat, acting as middleman in the supply of home produced stock for the table. As you are probably aware, most of what comes in at present is from the Continent, so I am able to undercut the imported stuff quite considerably. Anyway, I am already in negotiation with Tesco who are interested in some original hot food ideas of mine, but I'm thinking now about a cold food initiative that would suit the trolley service.

I have come up with Horse D'Ouevres©, a simple enough concept for what would just be lean slices of horse in a sandwich with the usual accompaniments. The cold range could be extended further with, for example, Gallop Pie©, minced horse with gelatin in a crusty pie with hard-boiled egg at its centre. And there are others. Do you think that the palates of your customers would be ready for this sort of fare? Apart from the railway themeing opportunities being endless, I can assure you that the product itself is quite delicious.

117

Do let me know what you think. Perhaps you could put me in touch with your current trolley service contractor?

Yours sincerely,

Ralph Tritt
MANAGING DIRECTOR

16 Sinclair Gardens,
London
W14 0AT

National Canine Defence League,
17 Wakley Street,
London
EC1V 7RQ

4th December, 2000

Dear Sir/Madam,

I wonder if I could ask your opinion in the course of some market research that I am carrying out with regard to a new dog related product?

My associate, Mr. Perry Edgbaston, has come up with an idea that I think could revolutionise dog handling, making the leash a thing of the past. The product, which we are calling Dog Cuffs©, consists of adjustable straps that attach to the animal's legs and restrict its gait accordingly. We have made a prototype from an old shoulder bag using velcro fastenings and conducted extensive trials with Mr. Edgbaston's own terrier bitch, Davina. After a few early tumbles, the dog soon learnt how to control its movements and stay to heel. Furthermore, with the straps fully braced, it is possible to "park" the dog outside a shop or other building regardless of whether or not there is a suitable tethering point.

We are at the stage now where we would welcome some professional input from organisations such as your own before applying for a patent. There may still be some refinements that we could make and, perhaps, there is a need also to try the device on some bigger breeds. In any case, it is something that we are both very excited by and believe will be a positive boon for dog owners everywhere.

I would be delighted to receive your comments and any practical advice that you might like to offer.

Yours faithfully,

Ralph Tritt

NCDL
National Canine Defence League

11 January 2001

Mr R Tritt
16 Sinclair Garden
London
W14 0AT

Dear Mr Tritt

Dog Cuffs

Thank you for your letter of 8 January enclosing a copy of yours of 4 December. As you rightly surmise we have no record or your earlier letter so it appears to have got lost in the post.

I find it difficult to visualise your product from your description. Do you have any drawings, photographs you could send which would enable us to evaluate its potential?

My one immediate concern is not specifically with your product but that the use of it might encourage people to leave dogs unattended in the street.

We do not condone leaving dogs tethered outside shops – where they can be subject to both interference and theft - at least they are generally safe from being run over. Your description of the Cuffs seems to suggest that a dog wearing them could, if sufficiently motivated, hop away from where it was left and thereby become an accident victim. Perhaps I have misunderstood this

If you are able to send some further information on tour product I will forward it to our Behavioural Administrator for his comments.

I look forward to receiving your reply.

Yours sincerely

Tony Brenton
NCDL Information Office

Cc NCDL Behavioural Administrator

17 Wakley Street
London EC1V 7RQ
Telephone 020 7837 0006
Fax 020 7833 2701
DX 400201 Finsbury 2
www.ncdl.org.uk

A Dog is for Life

16 Sinclair Gardens,
London
W14 0AT

Tony Brenton,
National Canine Defence League,
17 Wakley Street,
London
EC1V 7RQ

14th January, 2001

Dear Mr. Brenton,

Thank you for your reply of 11th January with regard to Dog Cuffs©. I'm afraid that I am no draughtsman, so rather than attempt to draw the device I shall try instead to describe it to you in a little more detail.

The Cuffs are in two pairs and attach to the animal's fore and back legs just above the knee by means of velcro fastenings. These are, in turn, connected by a longitudinal running strap with an adjustable buckle at its centre. It is this strap that controls the dog's gait and, when fully adjusted, will immobilise it as required. For ease, the buckle also has a quick release mechanism.

After trials with my associate Mr. Perry Edgbaston's own dog, Davina, we recommend that the optimum settings for the Cuffs are established first indoors and the running strap marked accordingly. We have used synthetic materials throughout for the prototype.

I hope that this gives you and your Behavioural Administrator a better visualisation of the product. Where it will work best, I think, is with the elderly or infirm dog lover, lacking the strength to exercise proper control over their animal and who may well risk serious injury through the attendant straining at the leash.

Yours sincerely,

Ralph Tritt

Ref:- 3ITB034

NCDL
National Canine Defence League

22 January 2001

Ralph Tritt
16 Sinclair Gardens
London
W14 0AT

Dear Mr Tritt

Dog Cuffs

Thank you for your letter of 14 January which I have discussed with our Behavioural Advisor.

We still have a bit of a problem visualising the **Dog Cuffs.** We are still concerned that even with the legs 'immobilised' the dog could still move away from a shop front when the owner was inside.

We are also concerned that if the dog feels so constrained it might be aggressive towards or be the victim of aggression from other dogs.

I appreciate the intention of your invention but I cannot quite visualise how it improves on the halter type lead.

Thanks again for keeping us in the picture.

Yours sincerely

Tony Brenton
NCDL Information Office

cc NCDL Behavioural Advisor

17 Wakley Street
London EC1V 7RQ
Telephone 020 7837 0006
Fax 020 7833 2701
DX 400201 Finsbury 2
www.ncdl.org.uk

A Dog is for Life

16 Sinclair Gardens,
London
W14 0AT

Tony Brenton,
National Canine Defence League,
17 Wakley Street,
London
EC1V 7RQ

2nd February, 2001

Dear Mr. Brenton,

Thank you for your further letter of 22nd January with regard to Dog Cuffs. I was about to suggest that we meet up for a practical demonstration of the device, but I am sorry to say that circumstances have arisen which now make that quite impossible.

My associate in this venture, Mr. Perry Edgbaston, has since accused me of trying to muscle in on his idea and take all the credit. This is, of course, quite ridiculous, but it does mean that we are no longer on speaking terms and that, henceforth, I am washing my hands of any further involvement with the concept.

I regret also to inform you of something more distressing still. I understand that Edgbaston's dog has been injured on Wandsworth Common after a collision involving a micro-scooter. I do not know the extent of the injuries, but I understand that the animal was cuffed at the time and unable to move out of the way.

It only remains for me to thank both you and your Behavioral Advisor for your interest and help thus far. Whether or not you continue the correspondence should Edgbaston decide to contact you independently I will leave to your own judgement.

Yours sincerely,

Ralph Tritt

6 February 2001

Ralph Tritt
16 Sinclair Gardens
London
W14 0AT

Dear Mr Tritt

Dog Cuffs

Thank you for your letter of 2 February.

I am sorry to learn that your friend's dog may have been injured. It is particularly unfortunate that she was wearing the **Dog Cuffs** at the time.

However, this does indicate a possible shortcoming in the design – especially where a lot of vehicular or pedestrian traffic occurs.

I have not heard from Mr Edgbaston so perhaps he has reconsidered the whole idea.

Thank you for putting me in the picture and for bringing the device to our attention initially.

Yours sincerely

Tony Brenton
NCDL Information Office

Cc NCDL Behaviour Advisor

NCDL
National Canine Defence League

17 Wakley Street
London EC1V 7RQ
Telephone 020 7837 0006
Fax 020 7833 2701
DX 400201 Finsbury 2
www.ncdl.org.uk

A Dog is for Life

TRITT COMESTIBLES

"No Nonsense Catering"

16 Sinclair Gardens, West Kensington, London W14 0AT

Bernard Matthews,
Bernard Matthews Turkey Farm,
Attlebridge,
Norfolk

10th March, 2001

Dear Mr. Matthews,

As head of a small, independent catering company, I am always alert to the possibility of a fresh opening and, to this end, would value a small measure of your own input.

Earlier this year I decided to take a close look at the demand for horse meat in the capital with a view to undercutting what comes in from the Continent. I was, however, put off the scent by the lack of a willing supplier and the hostility of various animal fanatics. As a consequence, I have had to lower my business profile considerably and would appreciate your own discretion when dealing with this correspondence. I know that you are no stranger to run-ins with these so-called welfare people yourself and will understand my position.

Anyway, what with all of that and now this foot and mouth epidemic laying waste to everything with a hoof, I have decided that poultry - and more specifically turkey - is definitely the way forward. What with you being King Turkey as far as the UK market is concerned, the last thing I want is to be seen as stepping on your toes and, worse still, inadvertently reproducing one of your own lines. (Rest assured I have no intention of farming the things.) Aside from all that, to be blunt, I don't have the resources to risk court action. What I am proposing is the launch of a shaped turkey fritter seasoned with 18 (yes, 18!) different herbs and spices as part of my own "Gobbler" range. It is my hope that you have nothing like this already in production and that you will have no objection either to my registering the "Gobbler" brand for myself.

I write out of courtesy and would want to wish you continued success in your own pursuit of comestible excellence.

Yours sincerely,

Ralph Tritt
MANAGING DIRECTOR

Bernard Matthews P.L.C.

Registration No. 625299

Registered Office:
GREAT WITCHINGHAM HALL . NORWICH . NORFOLK . NR9 5QD . ENGLAND

Fax: (01603) 871118 Head Office
(01603) 872421 Sales & Factory

Telephone: Norwich (01603) 872611

Direct Line No. **(01603) 873715**

Date	27 March 2001

Mr R Tritt
Tritt Comestibles
16 Sinclair Gardens
West Kensington
LONDON
W14 0AT

Our Reference   DMR/NW/0267

Your Reference

E-mail   david.reger@bernardmatthews.com

Dear Mr Tritt

I am replying to your letter to Mr Matthews dated 10 March 2001.

Gobbler is not a mark we own. This mark has been registered to Unilever and covers meat and meat products. I attach relevant details as obtained from the Patent Office's website.

If you wish to proceed with the use of this name you would be advised to write to Unilever – meat and meat products do not strictly cover poultry, but there may be other clashes with their registration.

Registration in your own right could be difficult given Unilever's prior claim.

I apologise for the delay in responding. I trust the above information is useful to you.

Yours sincerely
for BERNARD MATTHEWS PLC

D M REGER
COMPANY SECRETARY

Enc (1)

Cc: Mr D J Joll, Managing Director

126

PATENTS • DESIGNS
The Patent Office
COPYRIGHT • TRADE MARKS

Copyright
Designs
Patents

Trade Marks

Contact Details   Search   Site Map

Home : Trade Marks : Database : Register

Trade Mark Details

CASE DETAILS FOR TRADE MARK NUMBER: 2115121

Customer Ref: CTM/GT/FB/APP/288

------------------ CURRENT DETAILS HELD FOR THIS TRADE MARK ------------------

Status: Registered

Mark Type:
                Word Only   Schedule of Goods: 4

Class : 29

Mark Text:
GOBBLER

Date Filed:
Date Progress Stopped: 08.11.1996
(Earliest) Priority Date: Next Renewal Date:
Priority Country Code: Registration Date: 08.11.2006
If series, Number in Series: Archived Date: 30.05.1997
                   001   Licensee:

Journal Section: Yes
  First Advert   Journal No:
  Registration   6162 page 1441   Publication Date:
    Renewal   6184   12.02.1997
     Expiry   16.07.1997
  Assignment
    Division
     Merger
    Removal
  Restoration

Specification of goods/services:

Class 29:
Meat and meat products for food.

Residence Country Code: GB

                        Effective Date of Assignment:

Proprietor: Unilever PLC
    Address: Port Sunlight
          Wirral   ADP Number
          Merseyside   0592535001
          L62 4ZA

    Agent: Unilever U.K. Limited - Legal Department
    Address: Unilever House   ADP Number
          Blackfriars   0592536001
          London
          EC4P 4BQ

------------------ HISTORICAL DETAILS HELD FOR THIS TRADE MARK ------------------

Sequence Date
Number   Effective   Staff History
                Id   Text

TRADE MARK REGISTERED

Sequence Number 006	Date Effective 12.02.1997	Staff Id	History Text

ADVERTISED IN FRONT PART OF JOURNAL

Sequence Number 005	Date Effective 13.12.1996	Staff Id RESHAN	History Text

AMENDMENT TO LICENSEE INDICATOR

Status: Awaiting Advert
Page No. of Advert:
Next Renewal Date:
Registration Date:
Licensee:No
Opposition Expiry Date:

Sequence Number 004	Date Effective 06.12.1996	Staff Id R1JFRA	History Text

READY FOR ADVERT

Sequence Number 003	Date Effective 05.12.1996	Staff Id R1TLON	History Text

DRAFT FIRST ADVERT

Goods Specification:

Class 29 : Amendment
Meat and meat products for food.

Sequence Number 002	Date Effective 05.12.1996	Staff Id R1TLON	History Text

FORMS LOGGING CONVERSION - STATUS EXAMINED

Sequence Number 001	Date Effective 19.11.1996	Staff Id DASGRI	History Text

APPLICATION DETAILS CAPTURED

Click here for a glossary of terms used in the UK register details or

Click here for a glossary of terms relating to international Trade Marks.
New Register Enquiry   New Text Enquiry   New Proprietor Enquiry

TRITT COMESTIBLES
"No Nonsense Catering"

16 Sinclair Gardens, West Kensington, London W14 0AT

Unilever UK Ltd.,
Legal Department,
Unilever House,
Blackfriars
London
EC4P 4BQ

28th March, 2001

Dear Sir/Madam,

I am head of a small, independent catering company and write with regard to the isssue of the registration of trade marks.

I am proposing the launch of a shaped turkey fritter as part of an original range of my own called "Gobbler", and wrote recently to Bernard Matthews as a matter of courtesy over use of this mark. The Company Secretary, David Reger, has since replied stating that the mark is in fact registered to yourselves. I have to say that I was more than a little surprised to hear this as I had always understood your core business to be detergent. Nevertheless, I am wondering now where exactly this leaves me?

Would you have any objection to me using the mark on the understanding that it related purely to my own turkey based products? Failing that, if I were to go with "Gobblers" instead, how would that sit? It is not my intention to ruffle any feathers here, nor do I have the resources to enter into lengthy litigation.

I look forward to hearing from you and will not approach the Patent Office until such time.

Yours faithfully,

Ralph Tritt
MANAGING DIRECTOR

Unilever

Unilever House Blackfriars London EC4P 4BQ
Telephone 020-7822 5252 Telex 28395 Facsimile 020-7822 5951/5898

direct line 020-7822   5043

Mr Ralph Tritt
Managing Director
Tritt Comestibles
16 Sinclair Gardens
West Kensington
London W14 0AT

facsimile 020-7822   5817

Our Ref: CTM/TD/UK/gobbler

Your Ref:

10 April, 2001

Dear Mr Tritt,

Re: Trade Mark GOBBLER in the name of Unilever Plc – Request for Consent by Tritt Comestibles

I refer to your letter of 28 March 2001 regarding the above matter.

I have referred this matter to my marketing colleagues and I shall revert back to you once I have received their response.

Yours sincerely,

Terry Daly
Assistant Trade Mark Manager
Legal Group

Unilever

Unilever House Blackfriars London EC4P 4BQ
Telephone 020-7822 5252 Telex 28395 Facsimile 020-7822 5951/5898

Mr Ralph Tritt
Managing Director
Tritt Comestibles
16 Sinclair Gardens
West Kensington
London W14 0AT

direct line 020-7822   5043

facsimile 020-7822   5817

Our Ref: CTM/TD/UK/gobbler

26 April, 2001

Your Ref:

Dear Mr Tritt,

Re: Trade Mark GOBBLER in the name of Unilever Plc – Request for Consent by Tritt Comestibles

Further to my letter of 10 April 2001 I have now had an opportunity to discuss this matter with my marketing colleagues who have confirmed that they are prepared to consider any reasonable offer for our UK trade mark rights in GOBBLER.

For your information our trade mark registration is not due for renewal until November 2006 and covers "meat and meat products".

I look forward to hearing from you.

Yours sincerely,

Terry Daly
Assistant Trade Mark Manager
Legal Group

Unilever PLC
Registered in London number 41424 Registered office Port Sunlight Wirral Merseyside CH62 4UJ

TRITT COMESTIBLES
"No Nonsense Catering"

16 Sinclair Gardens, West Kensington, London W14 0AT

Terry Daly,
Assistant Trade Mark Manager,
Legal Group, Unilever PLC,
Blackfriars,
London
EC4P 4BQ

30th April, 2001

Dear Mr. Daly,

I am in receipt of your letter of 26th April with regard to consent on the UK "Gobbler" mark.

Before making you an offer, am I right in thinking that the mark is not currently active and that Unilever are merely sitting on it? You will understand me when I say that with the launch of a new product consumer ignorance is imperative. If there are Unilever lines already in existence with the "Gobbler" brand then I can't see the association doing either of us any good.

Also, are you able to give me a ball park figure? If my bid were to be successful, would I have the rights until November 2006?

I look forward to hearing from you.

Yours sincerely,

Ralph Tritt
MANAGING DIRECTOR

Unilever

Unilever House Blackfriars London EC4P 4BQ
Telephone 020-7822 5252 Telex 28395 Facsimile 020-7822 5951/5898

Mr Ralph Tritt
Managing Director
Tritt Comestibles
16 Sinclair Gardens
West Kensington
London W14 0AT

direct line 020-7822   **5043**

facsimile 020-7822   **5817**

Our Ref: CTM/TD/UK/gobbler

3 May, 2001

Your Ref:

Dear Mr Tritt,

Re: Trade Mark GOBBLER in the name of Unilever Plc – Request for Consent by Tritt
Comestibles

I refer to your letter of 30 April 2001.

I have been advised by my marketing colleagues that the mark has been used in the UK in the recent past on a turkey based meat product but that this product is no longer on the market.

With regard to any possible sale of the trade mark registration by Unilever, we would regard an amount in the region of £5,000 as reasonable consideration for the exclusive right to use GOBBLER on "meat and meat products for food" in the UK. This trade mark registration is not due for renewal until 8 November 2006 and could be renewed for a further ten year period at that time for approximately £200.

If you are happy with the aforementioned consideration I am prepared to prepare all of the necessary paperwork to transfer the rights from Unilever PLC to Tritt Comestibles at the UK Trade Marks Registry.

I look forward to hearing from you.

Yours sincerely,

Terry Daly
Assistant Trade Mark Manager
Legal Group

Unilever PLC
Registered in London number 41424 Registered office Port Sunlight Wirral Merseyside CH62 4UJ

TRITT COMESTIBLES

"No Nonsense Catering"

16 Sinclair Gardens, West Kensington, London W14 0AT

Terry Daly,
Assistant Trade Mark Manager,
Legal Group, Unilever PLC,
Blackfriars,
London
EC4P 4BQ

8th May, 2001

Dear Mr. Daly,

In response to your letter of 3rd May, it is with some regret that I have decided against any further pursuit of the UK "Gobbler" rights.

To be frank, your proposal of £5,000 is way beyond my budget. It will make better sense for me to simply go with another mark, and as such have decided to call my product "Turkey Tonight".

Thank you for your consideration in this matter. I am sorry that we were unable to do business together.

Yours sincerely,

Ralph Tritt
MANAGING DIRECTOR

Unilever

Unilever House Blackfriars London EC1P 4BQ
Telephone 020-7822 5252 Telex 28395 Facsimile 020-7822 5951/5898

Mr Ralph Tritt
Managing Director
Tritt Comestibles
16 Sinclair Gardens
West Kensington
London W14 0AT

direct line 020-7822   5043

facsimile 020-7822   5817

Our Ref: CTM/TD/UK/gobbler

Your Ref:

10 May, 2001

Dear Mr Tritt,

Re: Trade Mark GOBBLER in the name of Unilever Plc – Request for Consent by Tritt Comestibles

I refer to your letter of 8 May 2001.

I note that you are now intending to use TURKEY TONIGHT as trade mark name for your product. However, I would like to bring to your attention that Unilever are the owners of UK trade mark registrations for CHICKEN TONIGHT, CHICKEN TONIGHT SIZZLE & STIR, LIGHT TONIGHT and TONIGHT (details attached). Furthermore, CHICKEN TONIGHT has acquired a significant reputation in the UK and I would therefore recommend against using TURKEY TONIGHT as such use could constitute trade mark infringement and/or passing off of Unilever rights.

If there is any remaining interest in GOBBLER then I would suggest that you make a counter-offer which I can then put to my marketing colleagues for consideration.

Yours sincerely,

Terry Daly
Assistant Trade Mark Manager
Legal Group

Unilever PLC
Registered in London number 41424 Registered office Port Sunlight Wirral Merseyside CH62 4UJ

TRITT COMESTIBLES

"No Nonsense Catering"

16 Sinclair Gardens, West Kensington, London W14 0AT

Terry Daly,
Assistant Trade Mark Manager,
Legal Group, Unilever PLC,
Blackfriars,
London
EC4P 4BQ

15th May, 2001

Dear Mr. Daly,

I refer to your letter of 10th May.

I am prepared to make a counter offer of £500 for the UK "Gobbler" rights. If this is not acceptable to your colleagues, then I will take my chances and run with "Tritt's Turkey Tonight".

I look forward to hearing from you.

Yours sincerely,

Ralph Tritt
MANAGING DIRECTOR

TRITT COMESTIBLES

"No Nonsense Catering"

16 Sinclair Gardens, West Kensington, London W14 0AT

British Turkey Information Service,
Bury House,
126-128 Cromwell Road,
London
SW7

15th May, 2001

Dear Sir/Madam,

I am a small, independent caterer looking to branch out with a couple of turkey based products of my own. I wonder, do you have a starter pack that would help with this sort of endeavour?

I am currently in negotiation with Unilever PLC for the UK rights to the brand name "Gobbler" and have in mind a shaped fritter as well as turkey in a tikka masala sauce. At the moment, my meat comes direct from the supermarket, hardly a viable proposition. What I need is a wholesaler who won't try to pass off a lot of condemned carcasses as fit for human consumption, whether it all ends up in a curry or not. How do you protect against this sort of thing happening when even a big company like Shipham's can get caught out? Also, if I were to think about cutting out the middle-man at a later date, what are the regulations with regard to keeping livestock and dispatching of same? I presume that clubbing is still the preferred method, but with all these directives from Brussels now it's difficult to know where you stand on anything!

I do hope that you can be of some assistance and have enclosed a large SAE for your trouble. Do you also help in matters of arbitration? I ask only because I fear Unilever may start to resort to bully boy tactics and I haven't the resources for litigation with such a big fish.

Yours faithfully,

Ralph Tritt
MANAGING DIRECTOR

Ralph Tritt
Tritt Comestibles
16 Sinclair Gardens
West Kensington
London
W14 0AT

21 May 2001

Dear Ralph

Many thanks for your letter and the stamped addressed envelope concerning your development of some turkey products.

You had lots of questions that covered a wide variety of issues. Rather than try and cover these quite technical and lengthy areas in a letter perhaps you could give us a call to discuss them in more detail. We would recommend you contact Maire Burnett at the British Turkey Federation on 020 7202 4760.

Good luck with your product development.

Yours sincerely

ELAINE ELLIOTT
British Turkey Information Service

Turkey/letters/rt 210501.doc

BRITISH
TURKEY
INFORMATION
SERVICE

www.britishturkey.co.uk
Bury House
126-128 Cromwell Rd
London SW7 4ET
Tel: 020 7244 7701
Fax: 020 7373 3926

QUALITY
BRITISH
TURKEY

Unilever

Unilever House Blackfriars London EC4P 4BQ
Telephone 020-7822 5252 Telex 28395 Facsimile 020-7822 5951/5898

direct line 020-7822 **5043**

facsimile 020-7822 **5817**

Mr Ralph Tritt
Managing Director
Tritt Comestibles
16 Sinclair Gardens
West Kensington
London W14 0AT

Our Ref: CTM/TD/UK/gobbler

Your Ref:

18 May, 2001

Dear Mr Tritt,

Re: Trade Mark GOBBLER in the name of Unilever Plc – Request for Consent by Tritt Comestibles

I refer to your letter of 15 May 2001.

I have discussed your offer with my marketing colleagues and have been advised that we are prepared to assign our UK trade mark registration for GOBBLER for £1000. Please confirm whether this is acceptable.

With regard to TURKEY TONIGHT, I would strongly advise you to seek independent legal advice before proceeding to launch any meat-based products under this name.

Yours sincerely,

Terry Daly
Assistant Trade Mark Manager
Legal Group

Unilever PLC
Registered in London number 41424 Registered office Port Sunlight Wirral Merseyside CH62 4UJ

TRITT COMESTIBLES

"No Nonsense Catering"

16 Sinclair Gardens, West Kensington, London W14 0AT

Terry Daly,
Assistant Trade Mark Manager,
Legal Group, Unilever PLC,
Blackfriars,
London
EC4P 4BQ

29th May, 2001

Dear Mr. Daly,

I refer to your letter of 18th May and counter offer therein.

It would seem that my suspicions are confirmed, to wit Unilever attempting to make a mug of a small competitor through rank profiteering.

I have consulted my independent legal advisor, Mr. Perry Edgbaston, and will be proceeding as stated in my previous letter.

Yours sincerely,

Ralph Tritt
MANAGING DIRECTOR

Unilever

Unilever House Blackfriars London EC4P 4BQ
Telephone 020-7822 5252 Telex 28395 Facsimile 020-7822 5951/5898

direct line 020-7822 **5043**

facsimile 020-7822 **5817**

Mr Ralph Tritt
Managing Director
Tritt Comestibles
16 Sinclair Gardens
West Kensington
London W14 0AT

Our Ref: CTM/TD/UK/gobbler

Your Ref:

31 May 2001

Dear Mr Tritt,

Re: Trade Mark GOBBLER in the name of Unilever Plc – Request for Consent by Tritt
Comestibles

I refer to your letter of 29 May 2001.

I am extremely surprised that you regard £1000 for a valid UK trade mark registration as "rank profiteering". Nevertheless, can you please provide me with full details of your legal advisor in order that I can provide him with the particulars of our trade mark/common law rights in CHICKEN TONIGHT and TONIGHT. This will enable him to provide you with sound advice on the serious risks associated with using TURKEY TONIGHT in the UK for meat-based products.

Yours sincerely,

Terry Daly
Assistant Trade Mark Manager
Legal Group

TRITT COMESTIBLES

"No Nonsense Catering"

16 Sinclair Gardens, West Kensington, London W14 0AT

Terry Daly,
Assistant Trade Mark Manager,
Legal Group, Unilever PLC,
Blackfriars,
London
EC4P 4BQ

5th June, 2001

Dear Mr. Daly,

I refer to your letter of 31st May.

It is not the £1,000 I object to, it's the sudden drop from £5,000 when you could see that I wasn't interested. You were quite clearly trying to make a monkey out of me over what is, effectively, a redundant mark and of very little value. I would say that I have every justification in describing the 80% differential as rank profiteering.

My advisor, Mr. Perry Edgbaston, is out of the country at present on urgent turkey related business. Rest assured that your correspondence is on his desk and will be dealt with as he sees fit. You should also know that I am seeking arbitration through the British Turkey Information Service.

Yours sincerely,

Ralph Tritt
MANAGING DIRECTOR

98 Fernlea Road
London
SW12 9RW

Friday, June 15, 2001

Terry Daly
Assistant Trade Mark Manager
Legal Group, Unilever PLC
Blackfriars London EC4P 4BQ

Dear Mr Daly

I handle the legal affrairs for Mr Ralph Tritt, (of Tritt comestibles) who I understand has been in contact with you concerning the purchase of a certain Turkey Related trade mark.

Mr Tritt and I have had several most satisfactory meetings on this topic and have produced a consultation document setting out our aims and goals for the aforementioned trademark. Please be advised that this document is purely for consultative purposes and does and should not be construed as an offer (formal or otherwise) for the mark in question.

Please read it through very carefully and revert to me with any comments you may have.

Yours sincerely

Perry Edgbaston

Enc;

Friday, June 15, 2001

Brian

You said it was all over, you gave me your word! Can you imagine how I felt when Patricia told me that she had spent the weekend with you at the Imperial hotel in Torquay?

Patricia and I have been married for over twenty years, and we've been through our rocky patches - just like everyone else The prostrate surgery has proved to be particularly difficult for both of us. Patricia has always been a very physical person and misses that aspect of our relationship.

It is even more hurtful when you my best friend should take advantage of me in this way.

Perry Edgbaston

Ps if you don't heed this, the Inland Revenue will be hearing from someone about your Double Glazing business in Reading!

Unilever

Unilever House Blackfriars London EC4P 4BQ
Telephone 020-7822 5252 Telex 28395 Facsimile 020-7822 5951/5898

Mr Perry Edgbaston
98 Fernlea Road
London
SW12 9RW

direct line 020-7822   5043

Facsimile 020-7822   5817

Our Ref: CTM/TD/UK/gobbler

19 June 2001

Your Ref:

Dear Mr Edgbaston,

Re: Trade Mark GOBBLER in the name of Unilever Plc – Request for Consent by Tritt
Comestibles

I refer to your letter of 15 June 2001.

It appears that the wrong document was enclosed therein and I am therefore returning this to you
and look forward to receiving your proposal regarding the trade mark GOBBLER in the near
future.

Yours sincerely,

Terry Daly
Assistant Trade Mark Manager
Legal Group

Unilever PLC
Registered in London number 41424 Registered office Port Sunlight Wirral Merseyside CH62 4UJ

16 Sinclair Gardens,
London
W14 0AT

Sardis Enterprises,
6 Redbridge Lane,
Ilford,
Essex
IG4 5ES

5th July, 2001

Dear Sir/Madam,

I am looking to break into the entertainment business as manager of a unique vocal act of my own devising. Having seen your advertisement in The Stage directory, you sound like the sort of people who go all the way to the top, and, as such, I would like to offer you the chance of exclusive representation. You won't be disappointed.

The Gargling Patels is, quite simply, a one off. It took me a while to pursuade Jamal and Rita at the local mini-market to be a part of it, but I finally succeeded! That was three months ago. Now their four children are also involved and we have the sort of close harmonies that the Bee Gees would die for! The present repertoire consists mainly of Bollywood show tunes and is performed a cappella. My plan, however, is to introduce more popular chart material (Robbie Williams, Atomic Kitten, etc) as well as some authentic percussion sounds. There is also the possibility of endorsement from a major mouthwashing brand (currently in negotiation).

The act seems to work on a number of levels. Some people find it funny, others strangely moving. Either way, such is the professionalism, it's impossible not to be affected by The Gargling Patels. Owing to physical demands, the set is restricted at present to thirty minutes only, and some engagements would be subject to the staffing requirements of the family business. I am sure you will understand that there has to be some degree of compromise during these early days, but that all of this can be changed very quickly given the right circumstances! We await your instruction!

(Please note that the contents of this letter do not constitute a contract and that the concept expressed within remains the intellectual copyright of the undersigned.)

Yours faithfully,

Ralph Tritt

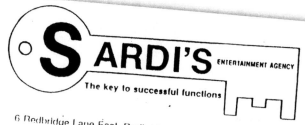

SARDI'S ENTERTAINMENT AGENCY

The key to successful functions

6 Redbridge Lane East Redbridge Ilford Essex IG4 5ES

Tel: 0(1)81-551 6720/1200

Fax: 0(1)81-551 1200

Ralph Tutt.
The Gargling Pakets

Date as postmark

Dear Artiste,

Thank you very much indeed for sending us the details of your act and we apologise if we have kept you waiting for a reply.

We have now put you on our files and are sure that we will be using you at some time in the future. In the meantime, if available, could you please let us have the following :-

C.V.   [ ]

Photographs   [✓]

Demo tape - Audio   [✓]

            - Video   [ ]

Date sheet   [ ]

Approx. fee   [✓]

Many thanks.

Yours sincerely,

Sardi's Enterprises

                              [ ] * PLEASE TICK HERE IF YOU
                                    WISH TO WORK ABROAD.

PLEASE COMPLETE AND RETURN TO SARDI'S - THANK YOU.

16 Sinclair Gardens,
London
W14 0AT

Derek's Doubles,
224 Commonwealth Way,
Abbey Wood,
London
SE2 0LF

15th August, 2001

Dear Derek,

I will be launching a celebrity-based book in London next month and am considering the hire of some lookalike types for comedic effect in a party environment.

Could you let me know who you have on your roster and the approximate cost? The party will probably be on a Friday, early evening for a couple of hours (in Mayfair). Would there be any sort of volume discount if I were to engage, say, a batch of six?

I look forward to hearing from you.

Yours sincerely,

Ralph Tritt

DERRICKS DOUBLES
224, COMMONWEALTH WAY, ABBEY WOOD, LONDON SE2 0LF
TEL/FAX: 0208 311 2129

Ralph Tritt
16, Sinccllair Gardens
London
W14 OAT

17th August 2001

Dear Ralph,

Further to your letter of the 15th August, we have pleasure in forwarding to you some of our posters. If you should be interested in anyone else please do not hesitate to contact us.

We would advise you that the prices start at £350 for a basic lookalike, tributes start at £400, plus travelling expenses and overnight accommodation should this be necessary. There would be no reduction for block bookings because each artist needs their fee.

We thank you for your enquiry, and remain,

Yours faithfully

Jean Whiting

J D Whiting

16 Sinclair Gardens,
London
W14 0AT

Jean Whiting,
Derek's Doubles,
224 Commonwealth Way,
Abbey Wood,
London
SE2 0LF

23rd August, 2001

Dear Jean,

Thank you very much for sending me the posters of your lookalikes.

I have to say that I didn't expect them all to be quite so expensive. I thought there might be a sliding scale based on quality and demand. Your Gary Glitter, for example, can't be getting much business these days, let alone at that price.

I hope you will understand that the lion's share of the party budget is allocated to the catering and so I have had to revise my plan to have a batch of mingling celebrity lookalikes. I am thinking now of just a single "high-impact" lookalike instead and your Princess Margaret would seem to fit this bill. Can you confirm that her image has been updated to incorporate the wheelchair, arm-sling and dark glasses? (It won't work otherwise.) I'm thinking also that this stroke business would be good cover if she can't do the accent.

Thank you for your help thus far. Could you also confirm whether there will be a VAT implication to build in? You seem to be a big organization but there were no company details on your headed paper.

Yours faithfully,

Ralph Tritt

THE INTERNATIONAL DOUBLES AGENCY
224 COMMONWEALTH WAY, ABBEY WOOD, LONDON SE2 0LF

Ralph Tritt
16 Sinclair Gardens
London
W14 0AT

30th August 2001

Dear Ralph,

We are in receipt of your letter of the 23rd August, and thank you for same.

We would advise you that there is a scale of charges, in that some are a lot dearer, and if they are tributes they can be £1,000's.

We would advise you that we have been in contact with Margaret Phillips, our Princess Margaret 'lookalike'. She has advised us that she would be willing to appear in a wheelchair, but that she does not possess one, so you would have to supply it.

We would, also, advise you that we are not registered for v.a.t.

Yours faithfully,

Ray and Jean Whiting
Ray and Jean Whiting
Managing Principals

A GALAXY OF STARS JUST A PHONE CALL AWAY

TELEPHONE: 0181-311 2129 (&FAX) 0181-488 2644/5 0181 312 4550
MOBILE: 0956 262442 PAGER: 01523 122333
SEE OUR WORLDWIDE WEB SITE http://www.posers.co.uk/ent/ddub.htm
FULL MEMBERS OF THE NATIONAL ENTERTAINMENT AGENTS COUNCIL

16 Sinclair Gardens,
London
W14 0AT

Sardis Enterprises,
6 Redbridge Lane,
Ilford,
Essex
IG4 5ES

19th November, 2001

Dear Sir/Madam,

Re: The Gargling Patels

We had correspondence in the summer with regard to the professional representation of my act, the aforementioned.

I understood that you had our details on file should anyone wish to engage us, and wondered whether this was still the case as I have heard nothing from you since. To be honest, we are at the point now where we are having serious doubts about continuing, what with a mouthwash sponsorship deal failing to materialise and the daily demands of a retail business to contend with.

It would be good to know where we stand with you.

Yours faithfully,

Ralph Tritt
MANAGER

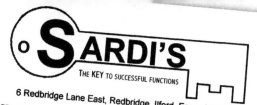

SARDI'S

THE KEY TO SUCCESSFUL FUNCTIONS

6 Redbridge Lane East, Redbridge, Ilford, Essex IG4 5ES

Telephone: +44 (0)20 8551 6720
Facsimile: +44 (0)20 8551 1200

E-mail: mail@sardisonline.com
Internet: www.sardisonline.com

Ralph Tritt,
16 Sinclair Gardens,
London, W14 0AT.

27th November 2001

Dear Mr. Tritt,

Many thanks for your letter of 19th November re The Gargling Patels.

We do have your details on file, and will use this act when the occasion arises, but up to now we have had nothing where the Gargling Patels can be best utilised.

From time to time the television people contact us for "out of the ordinary acts", and should this be the case in the future, we will certainly contact you.

Yours sincerely,

Maureen Shapiro

Partners: Mrs. M.L. Shapiro, M.R.E.C. and Mrs. W.F. Lewis, M.R.E.C.

SOCIAL TRITT

FOUR

16 Sinclair Gardens,
London
W14 0AT

The Manager,
The Ritz Hotel,
Piccadilly,
London
W1

18th January, 2000

Dear Sir,

I wonder if you have found a handbag probably left in one of the cubicles of your downstairs toilets? My wife often pops in to use them on her way to the bus stop and was in there last Saturday when she foolishly left it behind. It's black plastic with a gold coloured clasp, rather worn. There is no money in it (she always keeps her purse separate) just the usual woman's things. Her name is Frances Tritt.

I'd be obliged if you could let me know if it does turn up and I'll organise a jiffy bag for its return.

Thank you for your help.

Yours faithfully,

Ralph Tritt

21st January 2000

Ralph Tritt Esq.,
16 Sinclair Gardens,
London W14 OAT.

Dear Mr. Tritt,

Thank you for your letter of the 18th January. I have spoken with our Security Officer and I am afraid that no handbags were found in the Ladies cloakroom on the day in question. If by any chance it should appear at some stage I will of course let you know.

Yours sincerely

Luc Delafosse
General Manager

The Ritz, London
150 Piccadilly, London W1V 9DG
Telephone (020) 7493 8181   Facsimile (020) 7493 2687
The Ritz Hotel (London) Ltd. Registered in England No 64203C. VAT Registration No 420 4790 73

157

16 Sinclair Gardens,
London
W14 0AT

Canine Behaviour Centre,
Greendike,
Allendale,
Northumberland
NE47 9AW

19th January, 2000

Dear Sir/Madam,

Further to your advertisement, I would be glad to receive a free prospectus on the home study course in dog psychology.

I'm concerned that my two year old mastiff Van Outen might have developed what you people call an Oedipus complex. He is always mounting my wife's leg and goes for me in an extremely vicious way if I attempt to pull him off.

Hope you can help.

Yours faithfully,

Ralph Tritt

CANINE BEHAVIOUR CENTRE

Greendike
Allendale
Northumberland
NE47 9AW
01434 683162

21 January 2000

Mr Ralph Tritt
16 Sinclair Gardens
London W14 0AT

Dear Mr Tritt,

Thank you for requesting details of the Canine Behaviour Centre Dog Psychology Course.

As you will see from the enclosed Prospectus, the Course involves working at your own pace with questions at the end of each Unit so that you can monitor your progress. But there is also the option of completing six case studies, provided by us, for external assessment and validation. The Course is inclusive in that there are no books or materials to purchase.

I hope that the Prospectus answers all your questions but if there is any further information you require please do not hesitate to contact me or simply return the form to enrol on the Course. (Please note: a Course is dispatched within 14 days of receipt of the enrolment form).

I look forward to hearing from you.

Yours sincerely,

Deborah Bragg
Course Director

16 Sinclair Gardens,
London
W14 0AT

Deborah Bragg,
Course Director,
Canine Behaviour Centre,
Greendike,
Allendale,
Northumberland
NE47 9AW

26th January, 2000

Dear Mrs. Bragg,

Thank you for sending details of your home study course in dog psychology with regard to the problem involving my two year old mastiff Van Outen.

Unfortunately, the course is a little out of our range pricewise so my wife and I have decided to have the dog destroyed instead. (To be honest I think he was beyond psychiatric help anyway). We now have a tropical fish called Floppy Jack and life is far easier what with all the noise and mess before.

However, I have sent your prospectus off to Peter McKay at the Daily Mail who apparently has dog problems of his own. He is obviously a man of means so may well be good for a bit of business!

Thank you for your help.

Yours sincerely,

Ralph Tritt

16 Sinclair Gardens,
London
W14 0AT

SLP Ltd.,
Department TS/AB,
Admail 2175,
Llangollen,
North Wales
LL20 8ZY

22nd January, 2000

Dear Sir/Madam,

Further to your advertisement, I am interested in having my own amazing breasts and look forward to receiving your free catalogue.

Yours faithfully,

Ralph Tritt

S.L.P.

Medical Division

AMAZING BREASTS
CATALOGUE

CONE BREAS
miracle, se
ism for your

patient
ancer
th our
ique

tensive research and deve
ark has finally produced t
easts that are breathtakin

e real thing and
ied nipples. Miracle
, follows your movements up, down
without a bra. All bust sizes available, please
required. (GO BRALESS SEE PAGE 6)

Code SLP 500   Price £399 / $649

16 Sinclair Gardens,
London
W14 0AT

Inland Revenue,
375 Kensington High Street,
London
W14 8UA

30th January, 2000

Dear Sir/Madam,

I would like some advice on a query please.

I am interested in breast enhancement and have recently sent off for a brochure. If I was self-employed and working in the sex industry could the cost of this be offset against tax? By that of course I mean the cost of the breast enhancement and not the sending off for the brochure! (Although I suppose postage could be a legitimate expense also).

Thank you for your help.

Yours faithfully,

Ralph Tritt

Hammersmith 1 TSO
6th Floor
Charles House
375 Kensington High Street
LONDON
W14 8UA

Switchboard: 0171 605 9800
Fax: 0171 605

Mr R Tritt
16 Sinclair Gardens
LONDON
W14 0AT

Officer in Charge
G R Fraser

Direct Line: 0171 605 8108

Your Ref:

Date: 21 February 2000

Our Ref:

Dear Sir

I refer to your letter dated 30 January 2000 which I trust is a genuine enquiry.

I do not think that the expenditure would be allowable.   The general rule is that expenditure to allow you to work is allowable and expenditure which merely puts you in a position to work is not allowable.

The statutory legislation here is set down at Section 74 ICTA 1988 which states that for expenditure to be allowed it must be incurred wholly and exclusively for the purposes of th trade, profession or vocation.

If you wish to see a copy of the statutory legislation then please feel free to pop in to o Tax Enquiry Centre here at Charles House.

Yours faithfully

A THORP
HM Inspector of Taxes

915/EC/1/16.02/1770.doc

16 Sinclair Gardens,
London
W14 0AT

SLP Ltd.,
Department TS/AB,
Admail 2175,
Llangollen,
North Wales
LL20 8ZY

26th February, 2000

Dear Sir/Madam,

Thank you for sending me your Amazing Breasts catalogue.

I was keen on having a pair of my own until hearing from the Inland Revenue that the expenditure would not be allowable. According to Section 74, breasts are not wholly or exclusively required for the purposes of the sex industry.

Yours faithfully,

Ralph Tritt

16 Sinclair Gardens,
London
W14 0AT

North West London Newspapers,
Cumberland House,
Scrubs Lane,
Willesden,
London
NW10 6RF

24th January, 2000

Dear Sir/Madam,

I would like to place the following Valentine's Day message in the Chiswick And West London Guardian please:

I love your hot crevice juice dripping from my wang. Douche Boy.

I enclose a postal order to the value of £10 accordingly.

Yours faithfully,

Ralph Tritt

NORTH WEST LONDON NEWSPAPERS

Publishers of Kilburn Times, Paddington Times, Willesden & Brent Chronicle, Wembley & Brent Times, Brent & London Recorder, Wembley, Kenton & London Recorder, Ealing & Acton Guardian, Hammersmith & Fulham Guardian, Chiswick & West London Guardian.

☐ Cumberland House
80 Scrubs Lane,
Willesden,
London
NW10 6RF

Tel: 0181 962 6800
Fax: 0181 962 6899
AD-DOC DX 57666 HARLESDEN

Mr Ralph Tritt,
16 Sinclair Gardens,
London
W14 OAT

26th January 2000

Dear Mr Tritt,

Re: Valentine's Message

We are unable to publish your valentine's message, due to its explicit nature. Please find enclosed, your original postal order for £10.

Yours sincerely

John Hooker
General Manager

Independent Newspapers (Regionals) Limited, Head Office: 2 Whalebone Lane South, Dagenham, Essex RM8 1HB. Registered in England 366295

16 Sinclair Gardens,
London
W14 0AT

John Hooker,
North West London Newspapers,
Cumberland House,
Scrubs Lane,
Willesden,
London
NW10 6RF

31st January, 2000

Dear Mr. Hooker,

I am in receipt of your letter regarding my Valentine's Day message and your refusal to publish on the grounds of its explicit nature.

I have obviously been given the wrong impression by all the small ads in your paper offering the services of prostitutes and can only apologise for any misunderstanding on my part.

I have decided instead to go for national coverage and will be placing my message in the Daily Mail.

Yours sincerely,

Ralph Tritt

16 Sinclair Gardens,
London
W14 0AT

Daily Mail,
(Valentines),
Northcliffe House,
Kensington,
London
W8 5TT

31st January, 2000

Dear Sir/Madam,

I would like to place the following Valentine's Day message in the Daily Mail please:

Crevice juice wang douche.

The special person is my wife Frances and I would like the anonymous card to be sent to my home address.

Please find enclosed a postal order to the value of £10 accordingly.

Yours sincerely,

Ralph Tritt

Left margin fragments:

...ayer P.
...N'T forget
...are my pre-shiny thing
...ENEX.

...finity and be-
...rs Blip

B

...... I've seen
...our clothes on,
...ou in the nude,
...a cheeky little
...e can get quite
...and choice bird

BBY C. ♥
...o the moon and let
...among the stars -
...ee what spring is

...r and Mars' xx

...'s B.

...you lots, forever
...enjoy.

...ove you.

LOVE you to infinity
...yond....

BIG ears loves Bunny
...s much

IT never ends always

...love you

MINKY

Happy Valentines, Lots of Love Johnx

BOLA LOVE you forever Bavo

BOPS. MISS you hope all is well love Dribbles

BORKY LOVE you always Lady

BRIAN LOVE you lots from Bootsie Bunny Rabbit xx

BRIAN, STILL my Valentine in spite of your dodgy bits, love, Pat

BRIAN. I will always love you

BRIDGE ALL the world always!

BRONWYNNE PRINGLE will you marry me? from your favourite crocodile

BROWN EYES the rain it rainth all the day but my love for you shines bright

BROWNEYES, YOU are within my very soul, Ba-nanas forever, love you always, T

BREDA, LOVE you Madly

BRUCEY LETS go to bed. IGS

BRYONI ALICE love you lots Daddy

BUB ALL my love Bowler xxxxx

BUNCH LOVE you now and forever miss you loads cheers mate

BUNNEY LOVE cherish and adore you xxx Neddy

BUNNIE, YOU'RE my best friend, my lover, my every-thing; I have never, ever, needed or wanted, anyone, as much as I do you! Luv, H.B

BUNNY, LOVE and hugs from your Sister Gilly

BUNNY, LOVE you always Chickpea

BUNNY- TIME to seed the front garden? Baby Sausage.

BUTTERFLY YOU transform my life every day. melt me tonight. Snowman.

BIGAJA MON Amour Viki

CLANCY: MY love. Our hearts entwined forever: Princessx

CLARKIE BESTEST husband in the world love you loads Princess

CLIFF I love you darling Krystyna

COLETTE, ZOOM my heart went Boom.

COLETTE HAVE a Sensual Valentines, Love Jay

COLEY. MISS you Totty

COLIN YOU will always be my Valentine love forever M

COLIN, LOVE you, miss you. W.x

COUGAR BE my Valentine now and forever

COXY ELUSIVE but always gorgeous love you Mick

CRACKER- SUMMER in the

CRAIG, YOU always make me feel special, yours forever Laura.

CREVICE JUICE Wang Douche

CLARE SUDWEEKS We still love you even more than Newcastle United. Your boys.

CINDELLA. DONT eat the pd pies love from T& L& S.F.

CRW, TO the moon and back

CSGLP NO.7, always have always will. GLP

CUDDLES AKA Toffee Ba-nana. I'll always love you no matter what! NO MATTER WHAT!! Love Cookie

CUPCAKE EIGHT months on I love you even more togeth-er forever Lardy.

CURLY, LOVE you forever Peterxxx

CUSOON BIG guy.

CHRIS, I love you, Celia.

CHRIS, SNUGGLE close to me G.C!

Right margin fragments:

DEAR FFE Woo xxx

DEAREST as always

DEAR RAT

DEAREST precious ...gether. L

DEAREST mail 19... special ...you. D... love, Th...

DEARES love fro...

DEARES you for

DEARES CHINE... All my... MAN

DE...RE so ...oo Be..r.

DEAR... new ...all Mich...

DEAR yous...

DEB Gre...

DEB... glas...

DEB Ra...

DEB... eve

DEB yo...

DEB y... su...

DEB S... A... S...

A very personal message just for you

million

OTTE
xx

my
ever

October
nt a
to m
nge,

with
w w

TTI
. Ia

SSI
elie
ever

AND
r, all my love

LL New year
love, new li
of you, lo

CRUBS, I l
crubmaster.x
eb I love

rawl on b
Del Rooney

VE you

we have
ou, Al
S here Darling-

TH thoughts of
armed as by the
x
love you so much
National Newspa-
w everyone. Love

LOVE always. Em

ELY SEEKING

LOVE you always
il
Y strawberry sun-
es even better ten
Delish.
OUISE dreaming of
tantly
UEEN of Aley Green
ys love you JANxxx
LOTS of love and

thing
FIONA
Marry Me John
FIRTREE, MISSING,
you, Fairy
FIT BOD 22, fell in love with
your voice, your looks, your
personality but most of all I
fell in love with you. KMR
FLAPS I.L.Y always Bugs
FLASH. 'THE song has end-
ed but the melody lingers
on' Nelly
FLOSSIE, LOVE you to bits,
always have done and always
will do. Robert Redford.
FLOWER. NOTHING'S
changed. Always thinking,
always loving. Mouse
FLUFF I love you and will
miss you today Fuzzy.
FLUFF STILL love you! Fluf

HAIRY
HAIRY
horney alway
morny love for
HANNAH LO
money in the
xxx
HANNAH S.
tines', love
your Daily Ma

CHRIS
O'DONNELL
You

16 Sinclair Gardens,
London
W14 0AT

Penhaven Country House,
Parkham,
Snr. Clovelly,
N. Devon
EX39 5PL

21st February, 2000

Dear Sir/Madam,

I understand through the specialist grapevine that you will be organising a series of weekend breaks during the summer months especially for swingers.

Although my wife and I are no strangers to nudism, this would be our first time at actual swinging. Do you have an itinerary that would give us some idea of what to expect? Also, are there any age restrictions? (We are both in our early fifties with quite a lot of flab I'm afraid!) We prefer to bring our own equipment for hygiene reasons so that isn't a problem.

I look forward to hearing from you with further details on rates and availabilities and to securing an early booking. I trust also that I have your absolute discretion in this matter.

Yours sincerely,

Ralph Tritt

PENHAVEN COUNTRY HOUSE

RECTORY LANE PARKHAM Nr BIDEFORD NORTH DEVON EX39 5PL
Tel: 01237 451711 Fax: 01237 451878
E-mail: reception@penhaven.co.uk Web Site:www.penhaven.co.uk

25th February, 2000.

Mr Ralph Tritt,
16 Sinclair Gardens,
London W.14 OAT

Dear Mr Tritt,

Thank you for your enquiry today and we have pleasure in enclosing our brochure together with details of our "Special Breaks" for 2000.

We also enclose our Diary of Events for special Weekend and breaks this year.

When we started this hotel some sixteen years ago we looked to create a Country House Hotel that we would like to stay at - with peace and quiet, spacious attractive grounds to walk in, good food, an interesting selection of wines and professional, but friendly service.

Our three stars, excellent percentage and a Rosette from the A.A. together with Hospitality, Comfort and Restaurant Awards from the RAC and Egon Ronay listing leads us to believe that we have achieved what we set out to do.

We feel that we offer good value for money which is an important part of what we do and this is reflected by the very large number of guests who return to Penhaven time after time and both ourselves and our staff will work very hard to ensure that your stay with us will be a memorable one.

Yours sincerely,

MAXINE and ALAN WADE

16 Sinclair Gardens,
London
W14 0AT

Maxine Wade,
Penhaven Country House,
Parkham,
Nr. Clovelly,
N. Devon
EX39 5PL

6th March, 2000

Dear Mrs. Wade,

Thank you for sending me your brochure. You certainly have a lovely looking place.

I am a little confused, however, as you make no mention of swinging or address any of the questions I asked in my original letter. I appreciate the need for discretion in these matters but am not sure how to interpret your response. Are your weekend breaks special in the sense I think they are? Ditto your friendly and professional service? Or are we talking at cross purposes here? I'd hate to book up only to find myself a fish out of water.

Yours sincerely

Ralph Tritt

16 Sinclair Gardens,
London
W14 0AT

Berkeley Sweetingham Int.,
16 Hanover Square,
Mayfair,
London
W1R 9AJ

13th March, 2000

Dear Sir/Madam,

I assume from your address that you are an upmarket dating agency which is why I am interested in signing on.

Although not much of a toff myself, I am worldly wise and have just taken early retirement after thirty years with London Underground. I have a bit of money to spend and am determined to see out my autumnal years with a bang! It has been intimated to me that the sort of party girls you have on your books (debs and suchlike) are more likely to go with an older man like myself. I am also attracted by the prospect of civilised conversation and good manners, both of which being so hard to come by in these days of digital revolution.

I am taking this formal approach of contacting you as I daren't use the phone with my wife about. You can send your forms to this address as I always intercept the post.

I look forward to hearing from you.

Yours faithfully,

Ralph Tritt

16 Sinclair Gardens,
London
W14 0AT

Berkeley Sweetingham Int.,
16 Hanover Square,
Mayfair,
London
W1R 9AJ

22nd March, 2000

Dear Sir/Madam,

I wrote to you a few weeks ago requesting details on how to sign up but have heard nothing back.

I would appreciate a prompt response as I am having to intercept the post each day ahead of my wife who knows nothing of this.

Thank you for your discretion.

Yours sincerely,

Ralph Tritt

BERKELEY SWEETINGHAM
INTERNATIONAL

Ralph Tritt Esq
16 Sinclair Gardens
London
W14 0AT

24th March 2000

Dear Mr Tritt

Thank you for your letter of the 22nd March. Unfortunately we never act for people who are married and are therefore unable to help you further.

Yours sincerely

Virginia Sweetingham

Virginia Sweetingham
Principal

London Office: 16 Hanover Square • Mayfair • London • W1R 9AJ • Tel: +44 (0)171 408 9448 • Fax: +44 (0)171 408 9447
Country Office: Old Minster Lovell • Oxfordshire • OX8 5RN • Tel: +44 (0)1993 899 500 • Fax: +44 (0)1993 899 501
www.berkeley-sweetingham.com

16 Sinclair Gardens,
London
W14 0AT

The Big Issue,
57-61 Clerkenwell Road,
London
EC1

5th April, 2000

Dear Sir/Madam,

Just a few lines to congratulate you on your magazine. My wife recently brought home a copy from the launderette and it's the first time I've had occasion to read it.
I must say I thought it was very well put together indeed.

To be honest, I have been put off buying it in the past by those awful vendors you seem to make a point of employing and I wonder how many more there are like me who feel the same? I appreciate that the proceeds go towards homelessness but what sort of an advert is it to have people like that working for you? If you were to sell through a shop like normal publishers do then I think you would find that the extra cost would soon be recouped by far greater sales.

Anyway, you obviously mean well and I am happy to enclose a postal order for £5 for your worthy cause and to cover the cost of any more issues that my wife might happen to bring home from her travels.

Yours faithfully,

Ralph Tritt

Mr Ralph Tritt
16 Sinclair Gardens
London
W14 OAt

236-240 Pentonville Road
London
N1 9JY

tel **020 7526 3450**
fax **020 7526 3451**

14 April, 2000

registered charity no. **1049077**
company registration no. **3049322**

Dear Mr Tritt

Thank you so much for your kind donation of £5 towards the work of The Big Issue Foundation. I am delighted that you have chosen to help us in our work with homeless people.

Your support will help us provide real opportunities for homeless people to find and keep homes and jobs. Selling The Big Issue is often only the first step for many homeless people who hope to make a decent living and change their lives for the better. The Big Issue Foundation offers help with housing, drug and alcohol and mental health problems and provides jobs, education and training opportunities. Combined, these services offer homeless people the hand up they need to rebuild their lives and find permanent homes and jobs.

I am pleased to enclose a leaflet about the work of The Big Issue Foundation. Once you have read this it would be great if you could pass it on to a friend or colleague to spread the message about the Foundation's work.

Many thanks, once again.

Kind regards

L. O'Donoghue

Lynn O'Donoghue
Fundraising Manager

Enc

P.S. please do telephone me so that I can explain about our vendors to you. My direct line is: 020 7526 3457.

"Helping homeless people to help themselves"
The Big Issue Foundation. Registered Office: 236-240 Pentonville Road London N1 9JY

179

16 Sinclair Gardens,
London
W14 0AT

Glen Hoddle,
Southampton Football Club,
The Dell,
Milton Road,
Southampton
SO9 4XX

6th May, 2000

Dear Mr. Hoddle,

I will be retiring to Bognor Regis in the summer and want to settle a few things in advance of my move with your assistance.

As a keen follower of all association football, my nearest clubs will be Brighton And Hove Albion and Portsmouth City. Of course I'd much rather be a supporter at yours given its Premier division status, but the journey is prohibitive and I would need certain assurances before investing several hundred pounds in a season ticket.

My problem is severe congenital and progressive disablement. I would be arriving at the club under my own steam in a specially adapted people carrier and then transferring to a Shoprider electric scooter. Given these special circumstances I would require a pass for the executive car park well away from any crowds. I have my own on-board toilet facilities so that isn't an issue and I trust that the ground has proper ramped access throughout. But what about sight-lines once inside? Where exactly is your disabled section and would it be at all possible for me to park up somewhere on the pitch near the dug-out? Failing this, would the director's box be an option? Lastly, what are the chances of being invited back to any post-match hospitality and mixing with yourself and the players?

I hope you don't mind answering all these questions, but it is my experience in life that people are only too willing to accommodate the disabled providing you ask them directly. And what you don't ask for you don't get!

Come on you Saints!

Yours sincerely,

Ralph Tritt

SOUTHAMPTON
FOOTBALL CLUB
LIMITED

16 May 2000

Mr Ralph Tritt
16 Sinclair Gardens
LONDON   W14 0AT

Dear Mr Tritt

Thank you for your letter of the 6 May which was addressed to Mr Hoddle the Team Manager and has been passed to me for reply.

We appreciate your interest in supporting this Club as a season ticket holder but, regretfully, until we relocate to our new stadium in August 2001 we are unable to accommodate you.

The Dell is an old stadium with the smallest spectator capacity in the Premier League - a mere 15,250 - and our facilities for both able bodied and disabled supporters is limited. As it is we sell out for every game and have a long waiting list for season tickets.

Our new "St Mary's" Stadium will have a capacity of 32,000 seats and will have excellent facilities. However, as mentioned, we will not be playing at the new site until August of next year.

We are very sorry that we are not able to have your support next season but if you will let us know your new address in Bognor Regis in due course, we will send you the necessary information as soon as it is available.

Yours sincerely

BRIAN TRUSCOTT
Company Secretary

The Spirit of Southampton

Registered Office: The Dell, Milton Road, Southampton SO15 2XH
Telephone: (023) 8022 0505 (5 lines) Facsimile: (023) 8033 0360 Ticket, match enquiries (023) 8022 8575 (4 lines)
E-Mail: sfc@saintsfc.co.uk Website: www.saintsfc.co.uk
Company Secretary: Brian Truscott   Team Manager: Glenn Hoddle   Commercial Manager: John O'Sullivan
President: Ted Bates   Directors: R.J.G. Lowe (Chairman),   B.H.D. Hunt (Vice Chairman),
A.E. Cowen,   L.L. Gordon,   M.R. Richards FCA,   K. St. J. Wiseman   R.M. Withers
VAT Reg. No: 330 1812 08 Reg. No: 53301 England

16 Sinclair Gardens,
London
W14 0AT

Brian Truscott,
Company Secretary,
Southampton Football Club,
The Dell,
Milton Road,
Southampton
SO9 4XX

12th June, 2000

Dear Mr. Truscott,

Thank you for your reply of 16th May, 2000 with regard to the disabled facilities at Southampton Football Club.

I am pleased to say that I no longer have any plans to retire to Bognor since affecting a miraculous recovery.

God bless.

Yours sincerely,

Ralph Tritt

16 Sinclair Gardens,
London
W14 0AT

Freemasons Hall,
60 Great Queen Street,
London
WC2

13th May, 2000

Dear Sirs,

My father (long since dead) was taught to be cautious in the sixties and was a member of a Lodge in Manchester. As the son of a former Freemason, I am wondering whether this qualifies me for automatic selection or at least some sort of fast-stream induction process. Perhaps you would be good enough to let me know?

Having recently taken early retirement I am now looking to break into the world of publishing. Naturally I am keen to oil the wheels in any way I can and understand that being a part of your brotherhood is still the best way to do business on the inside. Funnily enough I still have my father's old kid leather apron, although his trowel disappeared some years ago after my mother left it out in a window-box.

I look forward to hearing from you.

Yours faithfully,

Ralph Tritt

United Grand Lodge of England

Freemasons' Hall, Great Queen Street, London WC2B 5AZ
Telephone: 0207·831 9811
Fax: 0207·831 6021

AJ/COMS/LITRI

16 May 2000

Dear Mr Tritt,

Thank you for your letter of 13 May. I am glad that you are showing an interest in becoming a Freemason.

Your comments lead me to believe that you may be interested in Freemasonry for the wrong reasons and I am therefore enclosing some literature, which I hope will enjoy reading.

If you are still interested in joining Freemasonry please could you write, explaining a little about yourself, directly to:

London Management
Freemasons' Hall
Great Queen Street
London
WC2B 5AZ

Yours sincerely

A Jackson
Communications Department

Mr R Tritt
16 Sinclair Gardens
London
W14 0AT

16 Sinclair Gardens,
London
W14 0AT

David Davies,
Football Association,
16 Lancaster Gate,
London
W2 2ET

20th September, 2000

Dear Mr. Davies,

I don't have to emphasize to you the importance of the England game against Germany on 7th October; not just as a World Cup qualifier, but as an affirmation that lessons have been well and truly learnt after the debacle of Euro 2000 and that we are back on the road to recovery.

God forbid that we should lose it (let's hope we can get another one in off the bar like in '66) but we all know what will happen if we do. The clamour for Keegan to go will begin again, and this time I think it will be hard to resist. The trouble is, who will replace him? Who would want to, for that matter? Might I be so bold as to suggest Jeff Powell of the Daily Mail?

Here's a man who really knows what he is talking about. He has the uncanny knack in being able to spot the limitations of a side even before it is picked, and that is to say nothing of his tactical awareness. He writes with huge conviction and quite clearly would relish the opportunity. Of course, his background is journalism and not football, but then that never stopped you. It's experience that counts, and Mr. Powell has seen it all. Besides, let's face it, footballers are a pretty dim lot. Don't get me wrong, Kevin Keegan seems a nice enough sort but he's never going to frighten anyone with his intellect. All I am saying is, maybe it's time to break with tradition and start drawing from a bigger pool.

Anyway, food for thought I am sure you will agree. As Don Revie used to say about football all those years ago: It may be a bladder of air, but it's bigger than all of us.

Yours sincerely,

Ralph Tritt

Our Ref: MS/DD/ENGM901

27th September 2000

Ralph Tritt
16 Sinclair Gardens
London
W14 0AT

THE FOOTBALL ASSOCIATION

PATRON
Her Majesty The Queen
PRESIDENT
H.R.H. The Duke of York

16 Lancaster Gate
London W2 3LW

Dear Ralph,

Direct Tel:
Direct Fax:

We refer to your letter in which you made comments and suggestions regarding the position of Head Coach to the England football team.

As we are sure you can appreciate, we have received many similar letters from a wide variety of people.

Jeff Powell may be an intelligent man who is undoubtably a highly qualified journalist. However, every single football supporter in the country has their own opinions on the selection of the England team, and Jeff Powell is one of the lucky few who gets to air his views to an audience of several million.

Irrespective of whether Kevin Keegan 'may never frighten anyone with his intellect' as you wrote, he is certainly a far more qualified candidate than most journalists. Kevin played for Liverpool, Southampton, Newcastle and SV Hamburg, won countless medals, was twice European Footballer of the Year, captained England, and won 63 England caps, scoring 21 goals.

I would think that most Premier League footballers were far more ready to work with, and respect the opinions of this man, than one who is paid to write about them and often criticise them.

This is by no means confined to Jeff Powell, but to every would-be England Manager in the country. The games start coming thick and fast now, with 2 Qualifiers in the space of 5 days. The build-up for Kevin himself couldn't have been any worse, experiencing the death of his mother early this week.

I am sure he will not hide behind this in the warm-up to the game, but if ever an England manager needed the support and backing of his fellow countrymen, it is now. So for one game, lets get right behind the team, and hope that the result against Germany is the one that we all want. Wouldn't it be fantastic to see some more positive headlines like we saw after the France friendly, and then 'intellect or not', we can be proud of the Manager and the players.

Yours sincerely,

Customer Relations Unit

The Football Association Limited Telephone 020 7402 7151 Facsimile 020 7402 0486
Registered Office 16 Lancaster Gate London W2 3LW Incorporated in London Registration Number 77797

16 Sinclair Gardens,
London
W14 0AT

Gerald Corbett,
Chief Executive,
Railtrack,
Euston Square House,
40 Melton Street,
London
NW1

5th November, 2000

Dear Mr. Corbett,

I thought that I should drop you a few lines of support after all the flack you have taken from the newspapers recently.

As a former employee of London Underground (30 years down he line) I do have some understanding of your position, although ticketing was my particular neck of the woods. People fail to realise that it is a business we are trying to run and simply chucking money willy-nilly at a problem will solve nothing. How quickly they forget the dark days of British Rail when it was the tax payer who had to subsidise this sort of chaos.

I had occasion to travel on the Great Western Railway last week from Bath to Paddington. The train was delayed by more than half an hour by speed restrictions imposed by Railtrack, but you would have thought by the moaning that I was the only man aboard who had any inkling of the safety implications of such an initiative. If a train is to be derailed at a black spot, then please God let it be travelling slow enough for human life to be preserved! The fact that I was unable to get a seat (not your jurisdiction I know) meant that I was also able to brace myself against the toilet door should impact have occurred.

What I am trying to say is that people will always have an axe to grind about something in this country as it seems to make them feel better about their own lot. I wouldn't take it personally. Now it's the weather and the fuel crisis that have taken over in the national consciousness and the heat is off. Really, when you've got your health, what else matters?

Yours sincerely,

Ralph Tritt

RAILTRACK

Gerald Corbett
Chief Executive

14th November 2000

Mr R Tritt
16 Sinclair Gardens
LONDON W14 0AT

Dear Mr Tritt

Many thanks for your note. You have no idea how helpful it is during this difficult time. The challenges ahead are immense.

Gerald M N Corbett

Railtrack PLC Railtrack House Euston Square London NW1 2EE
Telephone 020 7557 8111 Facsimile 020 7557 9024
DX 133075 EUSTON 3

Railtrack PLC Registered Office Railtrack House Euston Square London NW1 2EE Registered in England and Wales No. 2904587 http://www.railtrack.co.uk

16 Sinclair Gardens,
London
W14 0AT

The Kennel Club,
1-5 Clarges Street,
London
W1Y

5th November, 2000

Dear Sir/Madam,

My wife and I were obliged earlier this year to have our two year old mastiff, Van Outen, destroyed on medical grounds. We would like to donate his old kennel to your Christmas appeal.

It is approximately 3 feet long by 2 feet wide and 3 feet high at the apex. It was especially constructed by our neighbour, Mr. Perry Edgbaston, using ¾ inch tongued and grooved plywood screwed to a 2 by 1 inch pitch pine frame. The roof is lined with water resistant felt and the whole treated with preservative throughout.

I am at home most of the time, having recently taken early retirement, so you may collect the kennel at your own convenience. Please let me know when I can expect your truck.

It is a comfort to know that Van Outen's old home will be of some use to another.

Yours faithfully,

Ralph Tritt

THE KENNEL CLUB

1-5 Clarges Street, Piccadilly, London W1Y 8AB

Mr R Tritt
16 Sinclair Gardens
London
W14 0AT

09 November 2000

Dear Mr Tritt

Thank you for your letter 5 November regarding a donation of your late dogs Kennel.

We regret to advise you that we are very grateful for the offer, but we do not have a Christmas appeal. You may like to contact the RSPCA, NCDL or Battersea to see whether they would like the kennel.

We would like to thank you once again for the kind offer.

Yours sincerely

Melissa Hills (Miss)
Information Officer

Email: mhills@the-kennel-club.org.uk

Telephone: 0870 6066750
Insurance: 01372 743472 Library: 020 7518 1009 Fax: 020 7518 1058
email: info@the-kennel-club.org.uk internet: www.the-kennel-club.org.uk

190

16 Sinclair Gardens,
London
W14 0AT

The Secretary,
Royal Automobile Club,
89-91 Pall Mall,
London
SW1Y

6th December, 2000

Dear Sir,

I wish to bring to your attention the wilful and malicious flouting of etiquette that seems to prevail at your establishment.

As the guest of a member the other evening (I shall spare him the embarrassment by not naming him), I was alarmed to see visitors to the lavatory continually walking through the long bar without their jackets. When I followed one persistent offender in to remonstrate, he had the affrontery to say that he'd only one kidney and that people like myself should count their blessings and piss off back to the Garrick!

I have to say that the purpose of my visit was with a view to being proposed for membership. This is something about which, without reassurance, I shall now be having severe misgivings.

Yours faithfully,

Ralph Tritt

CDP/mem

19 December 2000

R Tritt Esq
16 Sinclair Gardens
London
W14 0AT

Dear Mr Tritt

Thank you for your letter of 6 December and I apologise for the delay in responding.

The Secretary, Mr George Kennedy, is currently away on holiday, but I will pass on your letter to him for his information on his return.

I am sorry that you had cause to take offence whilst visiting the Club. We do endeavour to ensure that the rules are adhered to at all times, and the staff are instructed to approach Members and/or guests who are not doing so. Thank you for letting us know that a problem occurred, and we will deal with it accordingly.

Yours sincerely

Carol Price
**Membership Secretary &
Head of Secretariat**

16 Sinclair Gardens,
London
W14 0AT

Valentines Messages,
Express Newspapers,
Classified Department,
4th Floor, Ludgate House,
245 Blackfriars Road,
London
SE1 9UX

29th January, 2001

Dear Sir/Madam,

I would like to place the following Valentine's Day message:

Put your lipstick round Ralphy's Trittstick, you big fat sow. Let me splash out on you tonight. Pearls before swine!

I would like the card sent to my wife Frances at the above address and enclose postal orders to the value of £20 accordingly.

Yours faithfully,

Ralph Tritt

EXPRESS NEWSPAPERS

Ludgate House 245 Blackfriars Road London SE1 9UX

020 7928 8000

Ralph Tritt,
16 Sinclair Gardens,
London W14 0AT

2nd February 2001

Dear Mr Tritt

Thank you for sending your Valentine's message (Daily Express ?) to us, unfortunately due to the content of your message we are unable to place it in the paper for you, if you wish to supply a new message I am enclosing a copy of your coupon together with a **REPLACEMENT BOOKING FORM** and an SAE for you to return it to me.

If you can pay by credit card, and would prefer, you can call me on **020 7922 2881** as I have the original coupon and can proceed once I have the necessary, new, information.

Many thanks.

Yours Sincerely

Fiona M. E Corallini
Express Newspapers
Advertising Systems Manager

16 Sinclair Gardens,
London
W14 0AT,

Fiona Corallini,
Advertising Systems Manager,
Express Newspapers Advertising Department,
4th Floor, Ludgate House,
245 Blackfriars Road,
London
SE1 9UX

5th February, 2001

Dear Ms. Corallini,

Thank you for your letter. I am sorry that my Valentine message is unsuitable for the Daily Express. It would seem that I have been given the wrong impression of your newspaper and can only apologise for any misunderstanding.

I am, however, quite happy for you to place my message in the Daily Star newspaper of the year. All the other details remain the same and I enclose postal orders to the value of £20 as before.

Thank you for your help.

Yours sincerely,

Ralph Tritt

Encl.

en we unite, our
rt and souls
May our love
forever. AAPKI

've already won
pite of me, don't
f I fall head over
be surprised if I
all that you are, I
lp it. xxx

GUIRE, I know
just how serious,
the time we had in
love PATRICK

ave and to hold. In
and in health. You
world to me. Love

Y KING, I love you
an anything, and
y for you, an invite
ial night, a party just
! Love 4 Eva,
OLY QUEEN ??

ve you, miss you, want
ed you, please be my
ne, MINDY

SIR Unconditional love
g about the stuff that
wear off. It doesn't
it lasts for all these
days, these crazy
, whether you're wrong
're right, I'm going to
ove you, still feel you,
e there for you, no mat-
hat, you will always be in
eart. Unconditional love.
KEISHA

ANTHONY you're never
e than a thought away.
e you forever, 'til the end
ime. THE MANCUNIAN

L BEAR Do you fancy a bit
Giggy Giggy? MR D BEAR

(PIGLET) We all love you
y much. Thanks for every-
ing. DAN, KAY, JAMIE
ND ALIBABE

BOUNCING BUNNY love U
ore & more each day.
hanks for being U, love from
our baby girl, CHELLE

DARLING JULIAN, its
mpossible to explain how
much I love you, but I can't
wait to show you on Friday !
All my love on Valentine's
Day - LINDSEY x x x

NATALIE, DARLING, SCOOBY
wants to marry you on 8th
December. Please SCRAPPY,
make SCOOB happy!

NATASHA, I love you, as always
& I'll be there for U. D ve
DARREN

NATBITE, hope you'll be my
Valentine. Love you forever
and always, CHIPSTICK xxx

NATE D, I love you loads, TC
xxxx

NATH - Here's to a New Year
and a new start, so don't let
me down ! All my love,
always, TASH xxxxx

NATH, Happy Valentine's Day,
love you with all my heart
and I wish you'd feel the same
way, love forever, GEORGE

NAUGHTY Not long till we're
together forever, can't wait,
Love WAYNE

NEIL BALDWIN, (Happy Valentine's, Babe, you're the one I
love and my best friend, its
wonderful sharing everything
with you, FNH x)

NEIL I do love you even though
I don't always show it. Happy
Valentine's Day. LOVE VIKKI

NERYS, You will be my Valentine's for the rest of my life, I
love you with all my heart
STUDMAN

NICE JUGS: Happy Valentine's,
love for all eternity, 4eva
yours, LOVE GOD

NICKY NOO NOO'S you mean
more than the World to me. I
will always love you. BRUTUS
BUBBA

NICOLA - the love of my life,
Happy Valentine's Day, see
you later, love you loads,
CHRIS

NICOLA DAWN CAREY, its now
for all to see, will you marry
me ? JOHN P

NICOLA JANE CROSS My love
for you grows stronger each
passing day, Love always
STEPHEN

love for you grows

PUSSYCAT, you ... looking
... ... my ... ooking
for ... rd to the 7th July. ... U
always, CHOO CHOO

PUT YOUR LIPSTICK round
Ralphy's trittstick, you big
fat sow. Let me splash out on
you tonight. Pearls before
swine!

R.J., I'm finally naming the
date, 25-08-01, and its all
arranged, love you always and
forever, J x x x

RACHAEL Love you loads and
loads. TIGER

RACHEL BELL - I love you now,
always and forever, be mine O
Valentine

RACHEL You are the best. I'll
love you till my day of rest.
You are absolutely brilliant,
all my love, Paul.

REENA I love you lots and
forever - when are we getting
wed? Love you forever -
FROSTIE XXX

REESO, I love you for what you
are - mine. Forever and
always, 24/7 - MOUSE

REGAN, I love you and I would
really love to be your
"Valentine". I know its
impossible, but maybe, one
day.

RICHARD HENRY-JERSEY, To
a wonderful husband, happy
Valentines darling, love you
so much, my love always -
JOSIE xxxx

RICK, you and me forever, 381.
Love PAULA x x x

ROBBIE, you are the love of my
life, my only Valentine,
always and forever our love,
your Babe, ANN x

ROBERT, to someone really
special, I love you very much,
you have been my Valentine
for the last twenty months,
SHARON xxxxx

ROSES ARE RED These rhymes
are corney, thinking of you
makes me feel horny. Juicy
Lucy - unleash my dragon

ROSES ARE RED, Violets are
Blue, I want to have another
eleven years with you,

SHANE I love you more than all
the moon and the stars in the
sky. Thankyou for the
fantastic time we spend
together. Forever - SARAH
XX

SHARON Happy Valentine's
Day. My love for you gets
stronger and stronger each da
we are together. Love you lot
- SIMON

SHARON, I J C S L Y. DE

SHAZZY BEAR, please forg
me, I am sorry, I need y
forever, lots of love alwa
CARE BEAR x

SHELLEY BABE Hap
Valentine's Day. Love
loads for always. TAYLO

SHERYL I love you more t
ever before and always
forever and ever. Ha
Valentine's Beautiful. Al
love - KEV

SHOGGY No matter how
nor bad it can get,one
baby U should never for
love U so much from the
of my heart, and miss t
mad, when we are
Happy Valentine's Day..
BECKY

SIMON I love you mor
each day that passes.
you for loving me EMM
x x

SIRENE EPICEÉ au cor
princesse aux lèvres t
Ayan, perle de Venus.
tu m'eposer ?
admire, cupidon t'en

SISSY BOY, you will a
my Valentine even
your nappy, my love
your LITTLE SWA

SLOP I love you more
Love and kisses, T

STAVROS, my fi
Valentine, in the 12.
known you, my
grows stronger,
yours, SMIFFY

STE WEBSTER All
love so can we con
on my yellow subm
can be with each
days a week so

STEVE BIRCH, I lo
than words can sa
and be mine f
TRACEY

STEVE, SWEATH
been 4 wonderful
very much in lov
the last time, w
Love PET

AGES

you loads and
wait until June
ur Wife. Love
OOH

it to be part of
rever, love you
Y =x=

you 4 ever, love

YCHOPS   And
love u now, always
SIMMIE CHOPS

A, you are and
ll be my FOXY
e. HARVEY xxx

A MARIE SAVAGE,
best thing that has
ened to me. Happy
's Day, from your
Only.

A, a very Happy
e's Day and a very
0th birthday, lots of
UL and BOYS

ANN, a little verse. so that
e whole World knows, how
y love for you just grows
d grows, love COLIN

BEVERLY GWILYM Love U
ore than life itself. U com-
lete me love CHRIS

O BREN, love you, BILL x x x

O BRUCE WILLIS, aka Gary
Hinken - I love you more each
day x Lookin' forward to
Skopelos, love JOANNA H x

O CAROLEMy Darling wife, I
love you with all my heart
forever. ALL MY LOVE, PHIL

CEILIA Best Valentine's

TO KAZ Roses are
are blue. Wait t
see what I do! f

TO KEV Just to
and to thank
me what hap
like.

TO KIM (
M/CR) Lots
love from

TO KIM O
you tons
to kno
always.

TO KIRS
a bo
'Grea
time

TO
yo
'P
a
J

T

spondolick
Loveyou always.

TO LINZ Happy Vale
Day. Love you always
ever xxx

TO LIZ, I love you load
love, STU XXXX

TO LYN KERSEY Al
Happy Valentines
do make me hap
DAVID

TO LYNDSEY MUR
you more!!!!! xxx

TO LYNSEY M
sweetheart. Lov
and miss you
love - YOUR
GEEZER MAR

TO MAMA WEA
kisses to all
Love PAPA

TO MATT BAR
Happy Valen
you always
XXXX

TO MAUREE
I still have
I love yo
with all my ne

TO MICHAEL, Happy Valentine's Day, just a message
letting you know how much I
love you, loads of love,

Someone special has put a
Valentine's Day message
into the Daily Star on
14th February ...so don't
miss it, pick up the
paper on the day
...and every day!

DAILY STAR

Happy Valentine's Day

of love
Valentine
loads, m

16 Sinclair Gardens,
London
W14 0AT

Sir Alan Sugar,
Chairman,
Tottenham Hotspur AFC,
White Hart Lane,
London
N17

17th February, 2001

Dear Sir Alan,

Just a few lines of congratulation on your famous victory at the High Court this week.
I'm not a Tottenham supporter myself (Leeds United as it happens), but I am all for
the small man standing up for his rights against a popular press that seems to think it
can ride roughshod over the agendas of others with impunity.

Of course, the truth is that this man Powell from the Daily Mail is as thick as thieves
with old Terry Vegetables and his attack on you is quite obviously part of a vendetta.
To refer to you as a miser in his tawdry article was an appalling slur and, given the
circumstances, tantamount to racism. I understand that the Mail will be appealing, but
it will show them in a very bad light indeed if it meant depriving Great Ormond
Street of the £100,000 award you have so generously donated to them.

Well done, Sir Alan! Good luck for the future and continued success with your
electrical equipment.

Yours sincerely,

Ralph Tritt

Tottenham Hotspur

Chairman's Office

Mr R Tritt
16 Sinclair Gardens
LONDON
W14 0AT

23rd February 2001

Dear Mr Tritt

Thank you very much for your letter of 17th February.

I appreciate the kind comments contained in your letter and thank you for taking the time and trouble to write to me with your good wishes.

Best regards.

Sir Alan Sugar

League Champions
1951 1961

Winners of F.A. Cup
1901, 1921, 1961, 1962,
1967, 1981, 1982, 1991

League Cup Winners
1971 1973 1999

FOOTBALL & ATHLETIC CO.LTD.
MEMBERS OF FOOTBALL ASSOCIATION AND THE PREMIER LEAGUE
Winners of the "Double" F.A. Cup and League Championship 1960-61
The European Cup Winners Cup 1962-63 & the U.E.F.A. Cup 1971-72 & 1983-84
Registered Office: Bill Nicholson Way, 748 High Road, Tottenham, London N17 0AP
Registered Number, 57186 England

sportswear partner

16 Sinclair Gardens,
London
W14 0AT

The Secretary,
Fabian Society,
11 Dartmouth Street,
London
SW1

22nd May, 2001

Dear Sir,

Having taken early retirement not so long ago, I am finding myself all too often at a loose end. My wife has suggested I join a club and yours does sound as though it might be a bit of fun.

I wonder if you would be good enough to forward some information as to what it is exactly that you get up to and the price of subscription? I would also be interested to see a copy of the bar tariff as well as being made aware of any other additional costs, e.g. special dress or equipment.

I am enclosing a large SAE for your trouble and look forward to hearing from you in due course.

Yours faithfully,

Ralph Tritt

FABIAN

SOCIETY
11 DARTMOUTH STREET
LONDON SW1H 9BN

Ralph Tritt
16 Sinclair Gardens
London
W14 0AT

25 May 2001

Dear Mr Tritt

Thank you for your request for information about the Fabian Society.

The Fabian Society is both a think tank for the Labour Party and a membership organisation. With 20 out of 22 members of the Labour Cabinet, including Tony Blair, Gordon Brown, and Clare Short, and over 200 MPs, MEPs, MSPs and AMs, Fabians are now at the centre of government. It's the job of the Fabian Society to ask the awkward questions - to identify the problems the government will face in the medium and longer term, and to offer radical solutions now. Our programme of publications, conferences and meetings offers an unparalleled forum for political debate.

Members receive all Fabian pamphlets on publication and four issues of Fabian Review a year. The Review provides advance notice of the conferences and other activities organised nationally and locally. I enclose a copy of Fabian Review, and hope you will find it interesting reading. Further information about membership is given in the enclosed leaflets.

Please ring this office if there are any points about membership that you would like clarified. We hope that you will decide to join, and look forward to hearing from you.

Yours sincerely

Giles Wright
Membership Dept

TELEPHONE: 0207 227 4900   FAX: 0207 976 7153   E-MAIL: info@fabian-society.org.uk   WEB SITE: www.fabian-society.org.uk

GENERAL SECRETARY: MICHAEL JACOBS

16 Sinclair Gardens,
London
W14 0AT

Giles Wright,
Fabian Society,
11 Dartmouth Street,
London
SW1H 9BN

29th May, 2001

Dear Mr. Wright,

Thank you for the information with regard to joining your club.

Unfortunately, there seems to have been some misapprehension on my part. Being stuck in a room full of Tony's cronies sounds like a nightmare. It's sociable I want, not socialism thank you very much.

Save the pound!

Yours sincerely,

Ralph Tritt

16 Sinclair Gardens,
London
W14 0AT

New Ambassadors Theatre,
Box Office,
West Street,
London
WC2

2nd July, 2001

Dear Sir/Madam,

I wonder if you could provide me with some information with regard to your production of the Vagina Monologues?

I was most interested to see that Mariella Frostrup will be joining the cast from 10th July and would like to know exactly what her performance will constitute. Obviously it is vagina based, but will she be discussing her own as well as other people's? Also, will there be vaginas on display, Ms. Frostrup's included? I am assuming that there are no restrictions with regard to male admission.

Lastly, what price for front stalls and are there concessions for the retired? (I'm not yet pensionable). I've enclosed an SAE for your convenience.

Yours faithfully,

Ralph Tritt

- Front Stalls Seats are £30. (concessions £15)
- There are no restrictions to admittance
- There is no nudity.
- The Monologues are based on interviews with over 2000 Women; not the personal experiences of the Cast.

With Compliments

Please reply to address indicated:

☐ New Ambassadors Theatre | West Street | London WC2H 9ND | Telephone 020 75...
☐ The Ambassador Theatre Group Limited | Duke of York's Theatre | 104 St M...
Telephone 020 7854 7000 | Facsimile 020 7854 7001

www.newambassadors.com | Registered Office | Fairfax House | Fulwood Place | Gray's...

Facsimile 020 7836 8012 | Box Office 020 7369 1761
WC2N 4BG
Company Number 03120328

'SEX has never been funni...
or more poignant'
NEW YORK TIMES

THE
VAGINA
MONOLOGUES
WRITTEN BY
EVE
ENSLER

NOW STARRING 3
AMAZING WOMEN!

SEASON EXTENDED
TO 9 SEPTEMBER
new AMBASSADORS

MEDIA TRITT

FIVE

16 Sinclair Gardens,
London
W14 0AT

Jonathan Ross,
BBC Radio 2,
Broadcasting House,
London
W1A 1AA

18th January, 2000

Dear Mr. Ross,

I have just seen another picture in the Evening Standard of you and your wife showing off her enormous bosom somewhere. Not that there is anything wrong with that. On the contrary. But it did give me the idea for a good joke if you are up for it.

My wife is a big collector of celebrity photos, with more than a hundred. Because of our unusual name, I wondered whether you had one of you and your wife with her bosom out that you could sign something like: What A Great Pair Of Tritts! Ralph And Frances! I know it would really make her day if you could. I have enclosed an SAE for your trouble.

All the breast!

Ralph Tritt

Music Entertainment Department
Radio 2 Production

Mr R Tritt
16 Sinclair Gardens
London
W14 0AT

19th January 2000

Dear Ralph,

Many thanks for your letter dated 18th January. In it, you mentioned you had seen a local newspaper article in your local paper about Jonathan and his wife and was looking for a similar signed copy as a gift for your wife.

Unfortunately, all these photographs are copyrighted to the individual newspaper and we're therefore unable to have one signed and sent to you.

As an alternative, I have enclosed a signed photograph of Jonathan which I hope will equally delight your wife.

Thank you for your continued support of the programme and thank you for listening.

Best wishes,

p.p. **Fiona Day**
Producer - Jonathan Ross Show

16 Sinclair Gardens,
London
W14 0AT

Peter McKay,
Daily Mail,
Northcliffe House,
2 Derry Street,
London
W8 5TT

26th January, 2000

Dear Mr. McKay,

Please find enclosed a prospectus for a home study course in dog psychology that might be of some use to you with regard to Tia your problem labrador bitch.

My wife and I were experiencing dog problems of our own until recently with Van Outen our two year old mastiff. We sent off for details of the psychology course thinking it would help but it is sadly beyond the reach of our pocket pricewise. Instead we have decided to have Van Outen destroyed and invest in a tropical fish.

However, I know you must be a man of means so this could be the very thing for you!

Good luck!

Best wishes,

Ralph Tritt

Telegrams, Daily Mail, London, W.8.
Telephone: 0171-938 6000

Northcliffe House,
2 Derry Street,
Kensington,
London, W8 5TT

23rd February 2000

Mr Ralph Tritt,
16 Sinclair Gardens,
London,
W14 0AT

Dear Mr Tritt,

Thank you for writing.

I am sorry I didn't write to thank you for the dog brochure. I was deluged with dog material following that article and some of the letters got detached.

My wife did find it very interesting, although whether or not it has led to an improvement in the mutt's behaviour is another question.

Yours sincerely,

PETER MCKAY

16 Sinclair Gardens,
London
W14 0AT

Michael Winner,
Style Section,
The Sunday Times,
1 Pennington Street,
London
E1 9XW

1st February, 2000

Dear Mr. Winner,

I was shocked to see a recent picture of you looking so fat but no wonder if what I read is true. According to Nigel Dempster you are eating five courses at a time in restaurants to see whether it is any good for your column. Surely you aren't supposed to eat it all? I know it is none of my business, but you have already had one bypass operation and I don't think they can do it again. Being a successful glutton is one thing, but there is no point in risking your health just because the food is free.

I mentioned this in a recent letter to John Cleese as I know he is a friend of yours. He didn't write back but did send me a picture of himself from that film of his that didn't do very well. I expect you must have quite a few of those yourself! Do you send out signed photos as well? I've enclosed an SAE for your trouble if you do. Funnily enough you look a bit like my father (although he is dead now). He was in films too but only as an extra. His best part was as a centurion in a film called Caesar And Cleopatra directed by Gabriel Pascal where he stood behind Vivien Leigh. Do you remember that?

Best wishes,

Ralph Tritt

SCIMITAR FILMS LTD.

Directors: *Michael Winner M.A.* (CANTAB), *John Fraser M.A.* (OXON), *M. Phil.*

PICCAD

Te

**MICHAEL
WINNER**

Dear Ralph

Thank you for writing to me. Your views about food-service-restaurants are very interesting.

I have passed your letter on to the Editor of the Style Section of The Sunday Times because it seems very suitable for publication. They may want to cut it a bit, I hope they will use it. The Style editorial people select the letters!

The book of Winner's Dinners is still on sale. It lists over 500 restaurants and hotels throughout the world, divided into easy to find countries and areas. It has my cartoons and other "delights!" I hope you might consider buying it!

Good luck and God bless ......

pic
encl!

MICHAEL WINNER

17.2.0

16 Sinclair Gardens,
London
W14 0AT

Michael Barrymore,
My Kind Of Music,
London Weekend Television,
Upper Ground,
London
SE1 9LT

19th March, 2000

Dear Mr. Barrymore,

Congratulations on your continued success despite all that hoo-ha over your private life. It just goes to show that true talent will always shine no matter what. I suppose it helps also that most of your fans are old ladies who don't seem to mind that sort of thing anyway. My wife is certainly a big fan and I have to say that I can't help but admire the way you work an audience. You really do have them in the palm of your hand with your funny movements and faces and they seem to laugh at anything at all. But then that's old people for you I suppose.

Speaking of palms, do you remember Madam Rosina the Torquay palmist? She was a fat old thing with a beard. She was always going on about predicting success for you when you were just starting out in summer season back in the late Seventies. My wife and I can recall seeing you at the Princess Theatre back then as we couldn't get tickets for Rod Hull And Emu who were on in Paignton. It's a pity really seeing as he's dead now. I wonder what happened to Madam Rosina? I expect her beard is completely white by now. In fact if you ever saw her again you could shout "Allwhite!" There's one you can use!

Anyway, do you do signed photos at all? It would be great to have one for old times sake. We haven't been back to Torquay since and I don't expect you have either. I've enclosed an SAE for your trouble.

Best wishes,

Ralph and Frances Tritt

212

Michael Barrymore

Tuesday, 28 March 2000

Dear Ralph and Frances,

Thank you for your recent letter to Michael Barrymore.

Michael has asked me to thank you for your kind words and to send you his very best wishes. I am also enclosing a photograph of Michael, which I hope you like.

Thank you once again for writing.

With good wishes.

Yours sincerely,

Michael Browne
Personal Assistant to Michael Barrymore

MICHAEL BARRYM

16 Sinclair Gardens,
London
W14 0AT

William Roache,
Coronation Street,
Granada Television,
Quay Street,
Manchester
M60

22nd March, 2000

Dear Mr. Roache,

Just a few lines to congratulate you on your recent performances in the nation's favourite soap. My wife and I are both thoroughly enjoying the Ken Barlow murder book story and eagerly await the denouement. It must be satisfying too for you as an actor to be able to really get your teeth into a story like this one and show off some of your range.

Would it be possible to ask for a signed photo? I've enclosed an SAE for your trouble. Is it true that you once worked with the late great Lord Olivier before you were famous? I seem to remember him praising you and speculating as to what might have been had you not decided to devote your talents to The Street all these years. Hollywood I suppose. The stage certainly.

Anyway, my wife and I are not alone I am sure in being delighted that you stayed where you did.

Best wishes,

Ralph and Frances Tritt

Mr & Mrs R Tritt,
16 Sinclair Gardens,
London
W14 0AT

June 28th, 2000

Dear Mr & Mrs Tritt,

Thank you for your letter and very kind comments to William Roache. I must first apologise for the delay in replying to you but your letter arrived at the studio just as William started a three month break and so you can imagine on his return the mail was considerable and I am just beginning to make headway with it. Anyway better late than never, I hope!

You asked about William's contact with Lord Oliver in your letter. He did go to him for advice when he first started his career in the theatre and Laurence Oliver, as he was then, told him not to give up and keep knocking on doors, which he did. Quite successfully. He never actually worked with him, although they met up several times over the years. After many theatre engagements William then went onto make four films and a great many television parts and the then, of course "The Street".

I hope this has answered some of your questions. I have pleasure in enclosing the autographed photograph and William sends you his best wishes and apologises for not replying personally but he is extremely busy with filming both "The Street" and a documentary about himself to be shown in December this year to celebrate his 40th year in "The Street". I hope that you will both enjoy this. By the way, The book 'Ken Barlow' has written is actually going to be on sale in the shops from July 31st!

Yours sincerely,

Sara Roache
Personal Manager

· CORONATION ST. ·

Granada Television Limited Registered Office: Quay Street, Manchester M60 9EA
Tel: 0161 832 7211 Fax: 0161 827 2004 Registered No: 840590 England

16 Sinclair Gardens,
London
W14 0AT

Lynda Lee-Potter,
Daily Mail,
Northcliffe House,
2 Derry Street,
London
W8 5TT

6th April, 2000

Dear Lynda,

My wife Frances and I have always enjoyed your forthright views and your column on a Wednesday is a real highlight for us. You always seem to hit the nail on the head as far as I'm concerned, but I suppose some people you are rude about are bound to take offence. My nephew has brought home pictures of celebrities in the nude that he has got from a computer including some of you. I can't believe that you would have posed for these so can only imagine that it is the work of someone getting their own back. It must be shocking for you but it seems as if this sort of filth is all that the internet is good for.

I do agree, by the way, with your thoughts on William Hague. He is not as daft as he looks. People can't seem to forgive him for being a clever dick at that party conference all those years ago, but I think he's the next PM.

Yours sincerely,

Ralph Tritt

16 Sinclair Gardens,
London
W14 0AT

Lynda Lee-Potter,
Daily Mail,
Northcliffe House,
2 Derry Street,
London
W8 5TT

6th May, 2000

Dear Lynda,

You must get so much post that I expect you probably won't remember the letter I wrote to you some weeks ago.

I wanted to congratulate you for speaking up on behalf of William Hague but also to voice my concern about pictures my young nephew had brought home from his internet of celebrities in the nude. Anyway, they appeared at first to include some of you, but I understand now that the images in question were in fact of Labour MP Mo Mowlam and I thought you would be relieved to know.

I can only apologise for any embarrassment this may have caused and for alarming you unduly.

Yours sincerely,

Ralph Tritt

THE DAILY MAIL

Telegrams: Daily Mail, London w.8
Telephone: 0171-938 6000

Northcliffe House,
2 Derry Street,
Kensington,
London, W8 5TT

15th May, 2000.

Mr. Ralph Tritt,
16, Sinclair Gardens,
London,
W14 0AT.

Dear Mr. Tritt,

Thank you very much for your letter. It was kind of you to take the time and trouble to write to me and I am of course relieved that there aren't pictures of me on the Internet! However, I do feel strongly about the potential dangers of the Internet, and clearly there is some dubious material being circulated, so it is in fact a subject I hope to be able to write about in the future.

In the meantime, thank you once again for your kind letter and I send you my very best wishes.

Yours sincerely,

Lynda Lee-Potter

DAILY MAIL IS A DIVISION OF ASSOCIATED NEWSPAPERS LTD. REGISTERED NUMBER 84121 ENGLAND & WALES

16 Sinclair Gardens,
London
W14 0AT

Mohamed Al Fayed,
Proprietor,
Harrods,
Knightsbridge,
London
SW1X 7XL

9th April, 2000

Dear Mr. Al Fayed,

My wife and I were both shocked to see you being made a monkey of by so-called comedian Ali G on television last night. It's a show we refuse to watch but happened to catch a glimpse of while changing channels.

You may not know it but this man is a fraud and a charlatan. He pretends to be a black man and then tries to make fools of his guests. His treatment of a man of your years and reputation was quite disgraceful, not to mention foolhardy. Is he not aware of your record in court? Perhaps you should remind him of it with a writ? Then we would see who was laughing!

I am afraid that this is yet another example of the decline in standards in this country and it is as galling for me as it must be for an overseas visitor like yourself.

Yours sincerely,

Ralph Tritt

HARRODS LIMITED, KNIGHTSBRIDGE, LONDON SW1X 7XL • TELEPHONE 020-7730 1234 • FAX 020-7581 0470 • www.harrods.com

17 April 2000   Chairman's Office

R Tritt Esq
16 Sinclair Gardens
LONDON
W14 0AT

Dear Mr Tritt

Thank you for your letter of 9 April 2000 addressed to Mr Al Fayed, he has asked me to reply on his behalf.

You may be surprised to learn that Mr Al Fayed thoroughly enjoyed his appearance on the Ali G show which he saw as a little light hearted fun, especially after his various battles which have been widely reported by the media over the last few months.

Once again, thank you for taking the time to write and for your kind words of support which Mr Al Fayed greatly appreciates.

Yours sincerely

Denise O' Sullivan

Registered in London No 30209 Registered Office 87/135 Brompton Road Knightsbridge London SW1X 7XL

16 Sinclair Gardens,
London
W14 0AT

Vicki Butler-Henderson,
Top Gear,
BBC Birmingham,
Pebble Mill,
Birmingham
B5 7QQ

10th April, 2000

Dear Ms. Butler-Henderson,

I am currently putting together a synopsis and 30 page text sample for Faber And Faber for a book based on my experiences with London Underground, working title The Complete Tritt.

As the book will be a combination of memoirs and specialist information (both procedural and technical) I have decided that a better title for it would be Bags Of Grunt, a phrase of course that you have made your own. I wonder whether you would have any objection to me using this? I am new to the publishing game and do not want to put anyone's nose out of joint or end up in litigation. I would be more than happy to give you an acknowledgement if you require one.

I have enclosed an SAE for your trouble as I know you must be busy driving like a maniac!

All good wishes.

Yours sincerely,

Ralph Tritt

21/4/00

Dear Ralph,

Charming of you to ask if you can use Bags of Grunt!! Tickled Pink!

Give it large my son!!

Best wishes for the synopsis,

Vicki Butler Henderson

VICKI BUTLER-HENDERSON
TOP GEAR.

16 Sinclair Gardens,
London
W14 0AT

Brian Sewell,
Evening Standard,
Northcliffe House
2 Derry Street
London
W8 5EE

20th April, 2000

Dear Mr. Sewell,

My wife Frances has quite a substantial Beryl Cook collection (mainly prints) with a recently acquired original entitled Nude Sun-bathers as its centrepiece. She will be holding an open day on the first bank holiday in May and I was wondering whether I could beg your indulgence?

Of course I know that you are much too busy to be expected to attend, but could you possibly spare a few words on the subject that I might type up and stick on a card? I don't know whether you are an admirer of Mrs. Cook but my wife sets great store by what you say (even though I'm sure she doesn't understand half of it!) and I know that your contribution, however small, would really make her day. She says that Beryl Cook is the Henri Rousseau of her day (although I think she used to run a guest house as opposed to being involved with customs).

I have enclosed an SAE for your convenience and would like to extend a big thank you in advance for helping out.

Yours sincerely,

Ralph Tritt

From BRIAN SEWELL

Evening Standard
2 Derry Street, London W8 5EE
Tel: 0171-938 6000

27 April 2000.

Your wife is in grave
error.

Brian Sewell —

16 Sinclair Gardens,
London
W14 0AT

The Controller,
Channel 5 Broadcasting,
22 Long Acre,
London
WC2E 9LY

26th April, 2000

Dear Sir,

I wrote recently to Gloria Hunniford complaining about the poor quality of reception on your channel but have heard nothing back. I don't suppose she has much understanding of this sort of thing so I can't say I blame her, but surely you must have something to say on the matter?

I know that Channel 5 is mainly what the newspapers call lowest common denominator television but surely picture quality is important no matter what you show? My wife and I have no interest in the mucky films or late night American rounders but we do like to watch Gloria's Open House in the afternoons. Sometimes the picture is so bad that we have to switch off. All that wobble starts to affect the eyes after a while and I understand that a lot of people in the country still can't get a picture at all.

Surely for any TV channel proper reception is the very minimum requirement? Particularly with all this digital technology that we hear so much about these days. Isn't that what it's supposed to be for? I don't pretend to be an expert in these matters but it does seem to be a funny way of carrying on.

Yours faithfully,

Ralph Tritt

Channel 5 Broadcasting Limited . 22 Long Acre . London . WC2E 9LY . Telephone 020 7550 5555 . Facsimile 020 7550 5554

Your Reference: DO/19769/MM

Date: 2nd May 2000

Ralph Tritt
16 Sinclair Gardens
London
W14 0AT

Dear Mr Tritt

Thank you for your recent letter.

Your postcode area suggests you should receive a Channel 5 picture from the Croydon transmitter, via your existing aerial. It's worth checking again to see that you've tuned in to the strongest signal in your area (channel frequency 37). If you are unsure how to tune in your TV, we suggest that you refer to your television manual which will give you clear step by step instructions.

You may also want to fit a signal booster to improve picture quality. These are available from most high street electrical retailers.

It may be that your existing aerial is not pointing at the transmitter which will give you the strongest Channel 5 signal in your area. Your aerial may therefore need adjusting or replacing. Enclosed is a list of aerial installers in your area who will be able to offer you the best advice on what needs to be done. We recommend that you ask for a quotation before committing yourself to any financial outlay.

If you are advised that you are unable, for whatever reason, to pick up a strong enough signal from the nearest transmitter, you could consider picking up Channel 5 via cable or satellite, or via one of the currently available digital options.

Please note that the contact details for the Channel 5 Duty Office are now as follows:

Telephone:	0845 7 05 05 05
Textphone:	0845 7 41 37 87
E mail:	dutyoffice@channel5.co.uk
Fax:	020 7550 5678

And the Channel 5 website can now be found at www.channel5.co.uk

Thank you for your interest in Channel 5.

Yours sincerely

Kate Allan

DUTY OFFICER

Enc: local aerial installers list

16 Sinclair Gardens,
London
W14 0AT

Mystic Meg,
Sunday Magazine,
News Of The World,
1 Virginia Street,
London
E1 9BD

26th April, 2000

Dear Mystic Meg,

This might seem like a strange request but could you tell me where you get your balls from? My wife Frances has a birthday coming up and likes to think that she has the sight as you people say. I want to surprise her with a crystal ball but haven't a clue where to find them. I expect the ones you use have been specially made or passed down through the generations, but do you know of a shop that supplies ordinary balls for beginners? My wife is not to know the difference as I'm sure you will agree a lot of this astrology is open to interpretation. In any case, I am quite certain she has never handled proper balls like yours before.

Also, would it be too much to ask for a speedy response? I know you must be busy but she's Taurus (11th May) so I don't have a lot of time to organise this. I have enclosed an SAE for your trouble. If you are sworn to secrecy about this or think that it is too dangerous for amateurs then I will understand. I am sure that a signed photo for inspiration would be almost as good if not better!

All the best for the future.

Yours sincerely,

Ralph Tritt

8th May 2000

Ralph Tritt
16 Sinclair Gardens,
London,
W14 OAT.

Dear Ralph,

Re: Crystal Ball

Thank you for your letter.   The best place to buy a crystal ball is at Mysteries, 9 - 11 Monmouth Street, Covent Garden, London WC2. Tel: 020 72403688.

Best wishes,

Janine Palmer

16 Sinclair Gardens,
London
W14 0AT

Loyd Grossman,
Masterchef 2000,
BBC Television Centre,
Wood Lane,
London
W12 7RJ

15th May, 2000

Dear Mr. Grossman,

Many congratulations on your latest series of Masterchef which has to be the funniest yet. It is the highlight of the week for my wife and I and never fails to raise a laugh. I am sure that there are many others who must feel the same. We particularly like it when the chefs do the droplets of sauce in different colours (or jis-plating as I believe the professionals call it) and marvel at how you remember all that French jargon and stuff we've never heard of before (or do you just make it up?).

I know that it is probably a bit late to ask but are there still tickets available for the studio audience? I've enclosed an SAE for your trouble. Is the seating unreserved? If not I'd like two near the front so my wife and I can get a good sniff of it. We've certainly never seen food like it anywhere else before or since.

Yours faithfully,

Ralph Tritt

LOYD GROSSMAN

Ralph Tritt
16 Sinclair Gardens
London W14 0AT

1st June 2000

Dear Mr Tritt

Thank you for your recent letter. Unfortunately, filming of this series of Masterchef has now finished but I am glad that you and your wife enjoy the show.

Yours faithfully

C Eadie

pp Loyd Grossman

16 Sinclair Gardens,
London
W14 0AT

Jeff Powell,
Daily Mail,
Northcliffe House,
2 Derry Street,
London
W8 5TT

2nd October, 2000

Dear Mr. Powell,

I have always been a great admirer of your forthright views, and it goes without saying that I find your columns required reading before and after any England game. And now here we are, poised for the next big one.

God forbid that we lose it, but if we do then the wee man Keegan (all heart and no strategy) will surely have to go. But who to replace him? Stand up, Mr. Powell! You know you have the wherewithal, and you certainly write as if you want it. Why not have the courage of your convictions and throw your hat onto the pitch?

I have already written to the FA stating your case for candidature and enclose a copy of their response for your information. The point I made to them is that football players are essentially dim and therein lies the problem. Being a former player should not have to be a prerequisite for management. After all, you don't need to be able to kick a ball yourself in order to know how it should be kicked properly. What we need are thinkers. People like you, Mr. Powell.

I don't suppose the FA will call you, but maybe it is time for you to make a call to them? You certainly have my support and that I am sure of many other Daily Mail readers.

Yours sincerely,

Ralph Tritt

Encl.

THE DAILY MAIL

Telegrams, Daily Mail, London, W.8.
Telephone: 020-7938 6000

Northcliffe House,
2 Derry Street,
Kensington,
London, W8 5TT

16 Sinclair Gardens
London
W14 0AT

29th November 200

Dear Mr Tritt

I guess they chose someone else! But if it comes back to an Englishman, then it has to be me or Terry.

Thanks again.

Yours sincerely

Jeff Powell
Chief Sports Feature Writer

DAILY MAIL IS A DIVISION OF ASSOCIATED NEWSPAPERS LTD. REGISTERED NUMBER 84121 ENGLAND & WALES

16 Sinclair Gardens,
London
W14 0AT

David Yelland,
Editor,
The Sun,
1 Virginia Street,
London
E19 9BZ

30th October, 2000

Dear Mr. Yelland,

Like most of your readers, my wife and I always look forward to a good chuckle in the morning over the front page headline and your cunning use of puns in The Sun!

We often try to see whether we can come up with something better and seeing your Oil Out War headline today about the fuel crisis has set me thinking. It must be tricky for your team to keep coming up with ideas, so what about a bit of help from your readers? This fuel business looks as though it will run and run, so here are a few headlines that I think you could use in the future.

• Oil For None And None For Oil

• Oil Hell Breaks Loose

• No Fuel Like An Old Fool

• These Fuelish Things Remind Me Of EU

If you like these, there are plenty more I can think of. Do you think there would be any money in it for me? I'd love to be able to contribute on a regular basis. I'm semi-retired now (30 years with London Underground) and could do with the cash.

Yours sincerely,

Ralph Tritt

1 Virginia Street, London E98 1SN Telephone: 020 7782 4000. Fax: 020 7782 5605/020 7488 3253

2 November 2000

Ralph Tritt
16 Sinclair Gardens
London
W14 0AT

Dear Ralph

Thank you so much for your headline ideas. They certainly gave us all a laugh!

We do in fact receive many letters suggesting headlines - though few are as good as yours - and I regret it is simply not possible for us to pay fees for them.

But thank you for writing, and I do hope you will continue to enjoy Britain's favourite paper.

With kind regards

REBECCA ROGERS
PA to The Editor

Registered Office: News Group Newspapers Ltd., 1 Virginia Street, London E98 1XY.
Registered No. 679215 England

16 Sinclair Gardens,
London
W14 0AT

The Editor,
Daily Star,
Ludgate House,
245 Blackfriars Road,
London
SE1 9UX

11th December, 2000

Dear Sir,

The Star has long been my newspaper of choice so it comes as some relief to see that standards haven't been allowed to drop since the takeover by Northern & Shell.

I know that there were some who feared that your paper would be dragged down market along with the Daily Express, but I see no evidence of that (although I can't speak for the Express as I don't buy it) and you are quite rightly newspaper of the year. However, I noticed today in the supermarket that the Daily Mail are also claiming to be newspaper of the year on their front page! How can this be so? I don't know whether they are deliberately trying to steal your readers, but surely it is one for the lawyers? They don't even have a proper page 3 or a pull out soccer section.

Anyway, keep up the good work. I know I won't be alone in making at least one suggestion. Can we have a few more Asian girls in the nuddy please? Cheers!

Yours faithfully,

Ralph Tritt

DAILY STAR

From the Editor

Ludgate House
245 Blackfriars Road
London SE1 9UX

Tel: 020-7928 8000

Ralph Tritt
16 Sinclair Gardens
London
W14 0AT

December 20 2000

Dear Mr Tritt

Thank you for your letter. I can assure that standards at the Daily Star will not drop, indeed standards will rise.

On the question of Newspaper of the Year, the Daily Star has been given this award by the Association of Circulation Executives in their international newspaper of the year competition. The Daily Mail won their newspaper of the year award in an entirely different scheme, run by the Press Gazette magazine. Our award was given last January. Their award was given this December. Their award runs out at the end of this year and I am hoping to add the Press Gazette Award to our other award in January 2001.

You ask for more Asian girls – if any apply to be Page 3 girls, I will gladly consider them.

Thank you very much for your interest in the paper.

Yours sincerely

Peter Hill
Editor

Facsimile: 020 7633 2044 Express Newspapers, Registered England No. 141748. Registered Office: Ludgate House, 245 Blackfriars Road, London SE1 9UX.

un A United News & Media Company

16 Sinclair Gardens,
London
W14 0AT

Gary Rhodes,
BBC Television Centre,
Wood Lane,
London
W12

2nd February, 2001

Dear Gary,

Just a few lines of congratulation on your latest series. My wife Frances and I are both great fans and can honestly say that we wouldn't mind eating some of the stuff you rustle up ourselves (which is more than I can say for a lot of the TV chefs!). It's all that oil and garlic we're not keen on, even when it's drizzled. Although we do like the Lawson girl on the other side.

I don't know whether you've tried them but we had a treat this week when we went "straight-to-wok" with some Amoy's Noodles. Anyway, for a joke I pretended to be you and painted on a widow's peak with shoe polish and did the French finger kissing thing as I served them up! My wife and I were in hysterics but I suppose you had to be there! Now I only have to do the French finger kiss and we both fall about. I hope you don't do it on TV next week! Especially if my wife has a mouthful!

Do you do signed photo's Gary? We'd love to have one of you to put up in the kitchen and I've enclosed an SAE for your trouble if you do. I know a lot of people say that there are too many TV chefs on at the minute, but we enjoy watching all that titivating with fancy ingredients and certainly wouldn't want to be bothered going to all that trouble ourselves. Life's too short to stuff a pimento as the saying goes.

Finally Gary, have you come across the new line from Ryvita called Currant Crunch yet? I happen to be "in" with the company and was lucky enough to get an early sampling. I have to say that they are a bit special and well worth checking out. Perhaps you could do something with them for next time?

Yours sincerely,

Ralph And Frances Tritt

GARY RHODES

Ralph and Frances Tritt
16 Sinclair Gardens
London
W14 0AT

20th February 2001

Dear Mr & Mrs Tritt

Thank you for your letter that I recently received.

Please find enclosed a signed photograph of Gary Rhodes which he has personally autographed for you.

He was very pleased to read that you are a big fan of his and I hope that you are enjoying his most recent TV series. I hope the photograph will inspire you to create some mouthwatering dishes and that it will take pride of place in your photograph album!

Best wishes

L. Kenyon

Lissanne Kenyon
PA to Gary Rhodes

16 Sinclair Gardens,
London
W14 0AT

Robert Kilroy-Silk,
BBC Television Centre,
Wood Lane,
London
W12

5th March, 2001

Dear Mr. Kilroy-Silk,

My wife and I would be interested in attending the recording of one of your programmes and I am enclosing an SAE for the tickets. Could we have a pair for the evening session? We only live a stone's throw from the studio but wouldn't want to be hanging around there first thing in the morning.

I have to say that I am a recent convert having retired only last year. To be honest, until I had the time to watch TV all day I had never even heard of you. I thought at first you were the chap from Cannon And Ball but my wife Frances says you were an MP, although she can't remember who for. Anyway, I expect that must come in handy when you have to pretend to be interested in some of those awful people you have on.

I know that you have had trouble with hoaxers on the show (it's amazing what some people will do to get on TV) but rest assured I am a no nonsense sort with plenty to say. My thirty years with London Underground should testify to that. My wife too is salt of the earth, although no stranger to strong drink!

Is there a list of subjects we can choose from for discussion? It would be good to know in advance just in case it's something we're not familiar with. You understand that we don't want to come across as idiots.

Yours sincerely,

Ralph Tritt

KILROY

The Kilroy Programme
2nd Floor Hart House
BBC Elstree Centre
Clarendon Road
Borehamwood
Hertfordshire WD6 1JF
Tel: 020 8228 7444
Fax: 020 8381 5786

12th March 2001

Dear Mr Tritt,

Mr Kilroy Silk has passed your letter onto me to reply to you – I am the audience co-ordinator. We thank you very much for your interest – our policy, however, is to book groups of people to come along to the studios, for whom we organise some transport. However, we are always looking for individuals to "make up the numbers" – particularly at short notice – on the occasion that the group we have invited has dropped in number. I wonder if you would be interested in this? My direct line is 020 8228 7463 – perhaps you might be able to give me a call and let me know if you would be interested in going on this "last minute" list? (I would have called you but there was no telephone number on your letter). I shall look forward to hearing from you.

Best regards,

Kate Timperley

KATE TIMPERLEY
Audience Co-ordinator

P.S. I have sent you back your S.A.E. so you can use it for another purpose!

ROY   Kilroy Television Company Ltd. Registered in England at 37 Warren Street, London W1P 5PD. Registered No. 2342140 V.A.T. No. 528 0826 42

16 Sinclair Gardens,
London
W14 0AT

Rupert Maas,
Expert,
Antiques Roadshow,
BBC Television Centre,
Wood Lane,
London
W12

6th March, 2001

Dear Mr. Maas,

Just a few lines to say how much my wife and I enjoy your performances on the Antiques Roadshow. You really do look as though you know what you're talking about, even if you are still learning the ropes. I suppose that's why they don't have you on very often, but I'm sure your time will come. To be honest, a lot of the others look like they should be put under the same dust sheet as Hugh Scully. And the sooner the better! Oy Michael! Which one's the antique?

We're not really ones for antiques ourselves (we prefer new), but my wife and I like to think that we know what's what and always seem to do well at guessing the prices. We once made the acquaintance of Arthur Negus at a car boot sale in Torquay. He was quite old by then, with a strong smell of urine and methylated spirits about him. He was never posh like you of course, but that didn't seem to stop him being an expert.

Do you do signed photos at all? We'd love to have one of you and I've enclosed an SAE for your trouble. Could you write "These Tritts Are Priceless" on it for a joke? I don't suppose there's much chance of the Roadshow ever coming to Shepherd's Bush Green. We do have something that might be of interest to you, a picture my wife picked up from Mencap some years ago. It looks a bit like the Mona Lisa except it's of an Indian woman. It has a white frame (probably not original) and I think the artist's name is Winfield. Do you know if he's collectable? I've not seen another like it.

Yours sincerely,

Ralph And Frances Tritt

British Broadcasting Corporation   Broadcasting House WhiteladiesRoad Bristol BS8 2LR Telephone 0117 974 2395 Fax 0117 923 7257
www.bbc.co.uk/antiques

Antiques Roadshow

Mr and Mrs Tritt
16 Sinclair Gardens
London
W14 0AT

20th March

Dear Mr and Mrs Tritt

Many thanks for your letter to Rupert Maas which has been forwarded to him.
I regret that we do not have photos of all our experts and we cannot supply
one of Mr Maas. There is a possibility that the Roadshow will take place at
the Horticultural Halls in Westminster later this year though it is only
provisional and likely to be postponed until 2002. If you are interested in
attending, please contact us later in the year or check our website,
www.bbc.co.uk/antiques.

Yours sincerely

Christopher Lewis
Executive Producer

16 Sinclair Gardens,
London
W14 0AT

Julian Clary,
It's Only TV But I Like It,
BBC Television Centre,
Wood Lane,
London
W12

2nd April, 2001

Dear Julian,

What a big hoot you are! My wife and I are both thoroughly enjoying the new series, so much so that we even watch the repeat on Saturday. You really are the king of innuendo (!) Or should that be queen?!

I have to say that your particular brand of homosexual humour is a long way from the limp-wristed sexist stuff that so tickled our funny bone back in the Seventies, and thank God for it! Who would have thought then that we'd all be rolling around at your cracks about semen and sodomy? And on the BBC! It just goes to show how far we've come and what an impact you and your ilk (elk!) have made in revolutionising light entertainment.

Of course, we're also huge fans of your close competitor Graham Norton (do you like him?) and were thrilled to get a signed photo and personal message from him recently (very rude!). I was wondering whether you could oblige with something similar? I've enclosed an SAE for your trouble.

Please give our best regards to Phil Jupiter, who has come on leaps and bounds. (We already have a signed photo of him.) A fat man is always good for comedy, especially if he's a cockney. What with Jonathan Ross and his funny mannerisms, it's little surprise that the three of you are such a hit. Keep it up! (The good work that is!)

All good wishes,

Ralph And Frances Tritt

Dear Tritts —
thankyou for your
kind words, + glad
to know you enjoy
my tired old jokes
featuring anal/oral
copulation
Best wishes
Julian Clary

Julian Clary

International Artistes Limited
Mezzanine Floor, 235 Regent Street, London, W1R 8AX. Tel: 0171 439 8401 Fax: 0171 409 2070

16 Sinclair Gardens,
London
W14 0AT

Independent Television Commission,
33 Foley Street,
London
W1

21st May, 2001

Dear Sir/Madam,

I understand that you are the people to write to when wishing to complain about an advertisement on the television.

I would like to bring to your attention the current campaign for Guinness that quite clearly contravenes your own guidelines by showing somebody who is intoxicated with alcohol. Although the advert goes on about some sort of dream club, the subject, a scruffy middle-aged man, is seen slumped at a table in a public house gibbering and hallucinating in a most disturbing way. He appears to be lost in a world of his own, quite destitute and with only alcohol to console him. To make matters worse, the commercial actually ends with a plea for us to join him!

Whilst I understand that we are living in a liberal society where anything goes, what is the point in having these guidelines if they are to be breached so flagrantly? Don't get me wrong, I'm no stranger to strong drink myself (although I won't drink stout), but these sort of negative images of alcohol are all too familiar in real life without having them thrust in our face in our own homes.

Yours faithfully,

Ralph Tritt

245

iTc

Independent Television Commission

Mr R Tritt
16 Sinclair Gardens
London
W14 0AT

04 June 2001

Dear Mr Tritt,

Guinness Draught - Dream Club

Thank you for your letter of the 21st of May. I am sorry that this advertisement has caused you concern.

We have received a few complaints about this advertisement, mainly relating to the surreal nature of the images, but we have not received any other complaints similar to your own. Inevitably with an advertisement of this kind interpretations will differ, but we are satisfied on current evidence that the main character is seen to be sleeping, hence the strange dream, rather than being portrayed in a drunken stupour. We do not believe that the advertisement is in breach of our rules.

Thank you for taking the trouble to raise this matter; the way alcohol is portrayed is an issue we take seriously and feedback from viewers is valuable.

Yours sincerely,

Elfed Owens

Elfed Owens
Advertising Complaints Officer

33 Foley Street London W1W 7TL
Telephone 020 7255 3000 Fax 020 7306 7800 Minicom 020 7306 7753
web site: www.itc.org.uk   email: publicaffairs@itc.org.uk

246

16 Sinclair Gardens,
London
W14 0AT

Elfed Owens,
Advertising Complaints Officer,
Independent Television Commission,
33 Foley Street,
London
W1W 7TL

7th June, 2001

Dear Mr. Owens,

Thank you for your reply to my complaint with regard to the current Guinness campaign on television. I am afraid that I must continue to take up cudgels with you on this one.

You say you are happy that the main character is asleep and not drunk and that the images he sees are a strange dream, yet the simple fact remains that he is slumped over a table in a public house! If this really is just about dreaming, why do we not see the man in a more conventional setting, like in bed or at ease in a comfortable chair? I put it to you, Mr. Owens, that if you see someone behaving like that in a public bar, then there is only one possible conclusion to be drawn, ever.

I fear that Guinness are pulling the wool over your eyes by dressing up a lot of pernicious twaddle as art. Or is it merely because they have so much money to spend on this sort of thing that nobody can afford to say no?

Yours sincerely,

Ralph Tritt

Ref: 38797
Direct Line: 020 7306 7712
Direct Fax: 020 7306 7717
email: andrew.carruthers@itc.org.uk

Mr Ralph Tritt
16 Sinclair Gardens
London
W14 0AT

3 January 2002

Dear Mr Tritt,

Your complaint about Guinness Draught advertising

I am sorry for the very long delay in responding to your further letter about this advertising. Although the points you raised were considered and your complaint reviewed shortly after you contacted us, unfortunately due to a backlog of casework it has taken much longer than it should have to write informing you of the outcome of this review. However, I am sure that you would, quite rightly, still expect a response.

Having reviewed the correspondence and the advertisement itself I am afraid that I have to say that we continue to believe that the advertisement concerned did not breach our Code of Advertising Standards and Practice. Let me explain why.

I accept that you feel strongly that the advertisement depicts someone who has collapsed through excessive consumption of alcohol. However, our role as a regulator requires us to view the advertisement as a whole and then form a view as to how viewers <u>in general</u> are likely to interpret the commercial. In this instance, we do not believe that viewers in general are likely to have shared your interpretation.

We think that the 'dreamer' in this rather surreal advertisement is likely to be understood by most viewers as just that, a dreamer or visionary, not a drunk. You question why, if the man isn't supposed to be drunk but only dreaming, the advertisement did not show him asleep in bed etc. The ITC does not have any role in directing advertisers as to which scenario to use to advertise their products. It was therefore a matter for them alone as to the choice of 'venue' for the dream sequence.

In any event, in order to take action against this commercial we would need to be convinced that the showing of it was, in very broad terms, likely to cause offence or harm to viewers or to mislead them in some way. We did not and do not believe that

33 Foley Street London W1W 7TL
Telephone 020 7255 3000 Fax 020 7306 7800 Minicom 020 7306 7753
web site: www.itc.org.uk email: publicaffairs@itc.org.uk

248

this is the case with this commercial. Specifically, we do not believe that any of our rules relating to the advertising of alcoholic drink have been broken.

In the circumstances, we therefore do not believe that we would have grounds for intervening against this commercial.

Once again, I am sorry has taken so long to notify you of outcome of our review. Let me assure you that this is not our normal practice.

Yours sincerely

Andrew Carruthers
Advertising Standards Officer

16 Sinclair Gardens,
London
W14 0AT

Shulie Ghosh,
Co-respondent,
ITN,
200 Gray's Inn Road,
London
WC1X 8XZ

22nd May, 2001

Dear Ms. Ghosh,

I do hope that I have spelt your name correctly. My young nephew, Peter, says that it is Indian for spinach, but I never know if he is pulling my leg or not!

Anyway, your name is very distinctive and you seem to cover just about everything that ever happens on the news these days, even presenting it when Mary Nightingale is off. I think that you would have been a far better example for Robin Cook to use in his speech about the positive affect of race in Britain. All this business about chicken tikka masala must be very embarrassing for you when, really, it's just a lot of muck they serve up in Birmingham.

Do you do signed photos at all? I'm not sure whether news people are allowed to do them. I've enclosed an SAE if it's possible. I have quite a distinctive name myself, but wouldn't make a very good co-respondent as I don't have the diction. Anyway, I'm retired now so any thoughts in that direction have long since passed me by.

Congratulations on your achievement, and please give my best regards to Nina Nannar when you see her. She's another one for the future!

Yours sincerely,

Ralph Tritt

200 Gray's Inn Road
London WC1X 8XZ
Telephone (020) 7833 3000

ITN

Many thanks for your kind letter.
(The Indian for spinach is actually 'saag'!)

With Compliments

Best Wishes

251

16 Sinclair Gardens,
London
W14 0AT

Trude Mostue,
Vets In Practice,
BBC Bristol,
Whiteladies Road,
Bristol
BS8 2LR

29th May, 2001

Dear Trude,

I wrote to you some time ago, but as I didn't have your full address you probably never received the letter. I am trying again now through the BBC even though you are not on at the moment.

My wife and I had originally planned to visit the South West earlier this month on a touring holiday, but thought better of it when this foot and mouth business started. Anyway, as it all seems to have blown over now, we'll be coming down towards the end of June instead and would love to include a visit to your place to meet up and perhaps get you to sign something.

I have enclosed an SAE for your convenience and wonder whether you would mind forwarding details of how to get there in the car along with a telephone number so I can make an appointment? Also, would we need to bring an animal with us on the day (we aren't planning to) in case the BBC are filming, or are there ones there that we can borrow? We wouldn't mind having to buy something small if it comes to that.

I do hope that the new practice has not gone bust. I suppose it makes for good TV either way, but we'd be disappointed not to see you.

Yours sincerely,

Ralph And Frances Tritt

Features Bristol

7 June, 2001

Mr R & Mrs F Tritt
16 Sinclair Gardens
LONDON
W14 0AT

Dear Mr & Mrs Tritt,

Thank you for your recent letter which was addressed to Trude Mostue. I am sorry that you did not receive a reply to your earlier letter. Unfortunately Trude will not be at her practice at the end of June as she will be away filming in America for a series called *Vets in the Wild*.

You will be pleased to know that Trude's practice is going from strength to strength. You will be able to see how she and Maria are getting on in the next series of *Vets in Practice* which will be broadcast sometime during the summer.

I am sorry that you won't be able to meet up with Trude while you are on holiday but I am enclosing a photo which I hope will make up a little bit for not seeing her in person.

Yours sincerely,

Jill Coster
Production Manager
Vets in Practice

16 Sinclair Gardens,
London
W14 0AT

Alastair Stewart,
London Tonight,
London TV Centre,
Upper Ground,
London
SE1 9LT

25th June, 2001

Dear Mr. Stewart,

I wonder if you would be so kind as to send me a signed photograph of yourself? I've enclosed an SAE for your convenience.

My wife and I both enjoy your performances on London Tonight tremendously and much prefer it to the BBC's Newsroom South East, which seems a little stiff by comparison. We particularly like the jokey moments you have towards the end of the programme involving the other presenters. I can see that there's a lot of banter going on and it's a wonder sometimes how you are able to keep a straight face. I suppose it's all down to experience, but it can't be easy for you keeping the knockabout stuff in check. I bet there must be some nights when you feel like mucking around throughout the whole programme! If only you could!

Do you know what happened to Katie Haswell? She was a lovely girl who used to do the late news up until last year, but now seems to have disappeared from our screens. They replaced her with the blonde (isn't that always the case?) who wears too much make-up and, I have to say, she isn't a patch on Katie. Oh, well. That's show business, as you people say. Or news business.

At least when it all comes to an end for you there's a real opportunity waiting in light entertainment. Dennis Norden won't last forever (although sometimes you wonder!) and I'm quite serious when I say that you'd be a natural in his shoes.

In the meantime, keep up the good work.

Yours sincerely,

Ralph And Frances Tritt

A LONDON NEWS NETWORK

THE LONDON TELEVISION CENTRE, UPPER GROUND, LONDON SE1 9LT. TELEPHONE 0207 827 7700. WEB SITE www.lnn-tv.co.uk

26. VI. 07

thank you very much. Katie is freelancing & we too see after a CNN!

Best wishes

WITH COMPLIMENTS

For Ralph & James –

best wishes

255

16 Sinclair Gardens,
London
W14 0AT

John Snow,
Channel 4 News,
124 Horseferry Road,
London
SW1P 2TX

26th June, 2001

Dear Mr. Snow,

My wife and I sometimes watch your news when there is nothing better on the other side and we've both spotted you cutting a dash with your fancy ties.

Do you have them specially made for the news? If not, would you mind disclosing where you get them from? I'm rather taken with the idea of getting one for myself, you see, in order to make an impression. If I did, would you advise keeping everything else plain, like the shirt and jacket? Perhaps you could send me a picture of yourself with one of them on for reference? I've enclosed an SAE for your trouble.

Mind you, I suppose you have to be careful not to go too far in case it interferes with the gravity of the occasion. It wouldn't do for you to have something really fancy round your neck if you were reporting a terrible disaster, for example, or something very sad. I can see that there must be a very thin line between being stylish and just downright offensive.

You certainly look like a man who knows how to strike the right balance, and that is why I would value your opinion.

Yours sincerely,

Ralph Tritt

Ralph Tritt
16 Sinclair Gardens
London
W14 0AT

4 July 2001

Dear Ralph Tritt,

Thank you for your letter of 26 June.

I must confess that I went for colourful ties because that avoided me having to buy endless shirts and suits and frankly I just go for what I like. Most of my ties are made by Victoria Richards who doesn't mind a call, mention my name, her number is ███████.

Best wishes.

Jon Snow
CHANNEL 4 NEWS

Registered Office 200 Gray's Inn Road London WC1X 8XZ Registered Number 548648 England
Independent Television News Limited

16 Sinclair Gardens,
London
W14 0AT

Independent Television Commission,
33 Foley Street,
London
W1

15th August, 2001

Dear Sir/Madam,

I would like to bring to your attention the blatant stereotyping that still seems to prevail when certain products are advertised on the television.

I refer specifically to so-called DIY products such as Thompson's Water Seal and Ronseal, and there are others. In each case, some sort of cockney oaf is featured shouting about the merits, as if these products were the sole preserve of people like that. It's actually quite patronising when you think about it. Who's to say that people who speak in this way are only fit to slap on a bit of varnish when they could just as well have a job in the City? Look at Jamie Oliver.

We all use these products, and that includes people from different origins and denominations. Let's put a stop to this nonsense and what is, effectively, just another form of racism.

Yours faithfully,

Ralph Tritt

iTc

Independent Television Commission

Mr Ralph Tritt
16 Sinclair Gardens
London
W14 0AT

Ref: 40053
Direct Line: 020 7306 7726
Direct Fax: 020 7306 7717
email: elfed.owens@itc.org.uk

02 October 2001

Dear Mr Tritt,

Your comments on stereotypes in advertising

Thank you for your letter of the 15th of August. I am sorry that the use of 'cockney' stereotypes to advertise some products has caused you concern.

We do not give prior approval to advertisements, the themes adopted, or the casting, but we can intervene if complaints or our monitoring suggest that there might be a problem. There are no rules about stereotypes as such, but we can act if there is evidence that the use of a particular stereotype is regarded by viewers as seriously offensive.

We have received hardly any complaints of this kind about the DIY advertisements you identify and viewers do not seem be be interpreting the accents used as having any special significance, or even being particularly stereotypical. They certainly haven't provoked great offence, and we couldn't justify intervention.

Thank you all the same for taking the trouble to give us your views. You might want to contact the agency, ADB (020 7878 5600), if you want more information about their casting policy for these advertisements.

Yours sincerely,

Elfed Owens
Viewer Relations Unit

33 Foley Street London W1W 7TL
Telephone 020 7255 3000 Fax 020 7306 7800 Minicom 020 7306 7753
web site: www.itc.org.uk email: publicaffairs@itc.org.uk

259

16 Sinclair Gardens,
London
W14 0AT

Ricky Gervais,
The Office,
BBC Television Centre,
Wood Lane,
London
W12

30th August, 2001

Dear Mr. Gervais,

Just a few lines of congratulation on your recent success. Your "Office" documentary seems to have gone down very well in certain quarters, although I have to say that there were very few laughs in it for me (and the audience, too, it would seem). No matter. It hasn't stopped you spreading yourself about of late and who is to say that you haven't earned it?

You probably won't remember me from some years back. I used to know you when you were at the University Of London Union in Malet Street managing those pop groups. Of course you were still called Norm in those days and always had that ginger girl with you. I used to work at Warren Street tube (retired last year) and would often take advantage of the cheap bar for a drink or three in the evening. Great times!

Anyway, it just goes to show that you never know what's round the corner. Giving up the pop music business is the best day's work you ever did. My wife was dead chuffed when I told her that I used to know you. Is there any chance you could send me a signed photo for old time's sake, Norm? I've enclosed an SAE for your trouble.

In the meantime, all good wishes for your next series (if there is one). You were always good value in the students' bar. Thanks for letting me in!

Yours sincerely,

Ralph Tritt

To Ralph
All the best
Ricky Gervais

16 Sinclair Gardens,
London
W14 0AT

Jimmy Young,
Radio 2,
Broadcasting House,
London
W1A 1AA

11th November, 2001

Dear JY,

Great news about the prog! My wife and I have been tuning in for longer than we both care to remember, so it was reassuring to learn that you'll still be with us after March 2002, God willing.

It's good to see also that people power still counts for something in this country (5 million listeners can't be wrong!). What age has to do with it I can't understand. There is certainly no evidence of it affecting your performance on air, and who's to know or even care how old you are when you are never seen? (Actually, my wife and I did see you once many years ago in Brixham, South Devon, broadcasting from the Golden Hind replica ship. I think it sank soon after, but they had it rebuilt using garden sheds.)

Any chance of a signed photo? I've enclosed an SAE for your trouble. At least you know now that when the time does come to hang up your headphones, Nicky Campbell won't be the one stepping into your shoes. After what he said I think he's definitely shot himself in the foot.

BFNYOC!

Yours sincerely,

Ralph Tritt

JIMMY YOUNG

13/11/01

Dear Ralph,

Thank You for
Your letter.

The "great news"
Has Been Considerably
Exaggerated By the
Press. I'm Not Safe
Yet, But I'm Keeping
My fingers Crossed

All the Best

Jim

16 Sinclair Gardens,
London
W14 0AT

Independent Television Commission,
33 Foley Street,
London
W1

28th February, 2002

Dear Sir/Madam,

I wish to complain in the strongest possible terms about the latest advert in the Sainsbury's campaign featuring so-called naked chef Jamie Oliver.

Why a commercial for Chinese food should give licence to such racist antics is beyond me. The portrayal of people from the Orient as cleaver-wielding kung-fu specialists is nothing short of offensive. As for Oliver's gobbledegook impressions of how they are supposed to speak, words fail me. It's the sort of pernicious stereotyping I thought had died out with The Benny Hill Show.

The makers, of course, will use humour as their defence. But what if Sainsbury's were to chose Caribbean food for advertisement? Would we then see Oliver blacked up in a loin-cloth and waving a spear? Of course not. So what is the difference, I ask you? Surely not colour?

Yours faithfully,

Ralph Tritt

Independent Television Commission

Mr Ralph Tritt
16 Sinclair Gardens
London
W14 0AT

Ref: 66091
Direct Line: 020 7306 7861
Direct Fax: 020 7306 7717
email: ian.parkes@itc.org.uk

14 June 2002

Dear Mr Tritt

Your complaint about Sainsbury's - Oriental Range advertising

Thank you for contacting us about this commercial. A number of viewers told us that they were concerned it was in poor taste or offensive. I have enclosed a copy of our adjudication but I wanted to explain our decision a little more.

Although viewers accused the commercial of being racist, we do not consider there was any intention to portray any race as superior compared to the Chinese. It was clearly intended to promote the Chinese New Year and celebrations and to encourage customers to join in with the celebrations by purchasing Sainsbury's pre-prepared oriental style food.

Some viewers objected to what they regarded as Jamie Oliver negatively stereotyping Chinese people by performing Kung-Fu moves and speaking Cantonese. When we were investigating the complaints we felt it was vitally important to find out what the Chinese community really thought. We therefore made contact with members of the community (who had recently been involved in quite a large internet discussion group about it) and they told us that the consensus appeared to be that it was perhaps borderline but not widely felt to be offensive.

They said that the Kung-Fu moves did irritate some, particularly because a white person performed them. However, they also said there was an appreciation that the advertiser had gone some considerable way to countering that by using a language coach to train Jamie Oliver to speak Cantonese as best he could. Our contacts told us that the use of genuine Cantonese speech and accurate translation at the end of the advertisement was seen as a redeeming feature to many of the Chinese community, with whom they had been in contact.

33 Foley Street London W1W 7TL
Telephone 020 7255 3000 Fax 020 7306 7800 Minicom 020 7306 7753
web site: www.itc.org.uk   email: publicaffairs@itc.org.uk

We have been told that other races wouldn't accept negative stereotypes. The viewers who have expressed this opinion pointed in particular to the Caribbean and Indian community. We do not ban the use of stereotypes outright. They can be useful to create an impression in a short space of time. However, we do insist that their use is carefully thought through and that they are not utilised in such a way as to promote or feed prejudice.

In this case although accepted that the advertisement was not to everyone's liking, we also accepted the positive message of the advertiser seeking to promote the culture and cuisine of the Orient. Looking at the complaints we received and listening to the contacts we made, we judged that the advertisement had not caused deep-felt or widespread offensive and did not uphold the complaints.

Thank you nonetheless for sharing your views and for your patience whilst we looked in to the case for you.

Yours sincerely

Ian Parkes
Advertising Complaints Officer

Harmful Sainsbury's - Oriental Range
Advertising agency: Abbot Mead Vickers

COMPLAINT FROM: 11 viewers

BACKGROUND: An advertisement for Sainsbury's Oriental range of prepared meals featured Jamie Oliver speaking Cantonese. He acted out Kung Fu-style moves as he cooked for friends. The advertisement was subtitled to translate the spoken Cantonese.

ISSUE: Viewers including some members of the Chinese community complained that the advertisement was offensive. They felt it negatively stereotyped Chinese people and their culture by suggesting that they all ate sweet and sour pork and practised Kung Fu. Jamie Oliver's attempt at speaking Cantonese was particularly criticised, one viewer said that "it came across as nothing better than what I often heard as taunts in the school playground".

ASSESSMENT: The advertiser said it had intended to celebrate Oriental cuisine and culture in a positive way and was concerned that some viewers felt the advertisement reinforced negative racial stereotypes. It explained that a Cantonese translator and language coach were used throughout the making of the advertisement to ensure that subtitles and Jamie Oliver's pronunciation were accurate and authentic. The BACC did not believe that the "Kung Fu" scenes presented a negative stereotype of the Chinese community. It argued that it was intended as a tribute to films such as Crouching Tiger Hidden Dragon. Although it acknowledged that Chinese culture was diverse, BACC felt it was acceptable for an advertisement to reflect this one aspect of the culture provided that it was not presented in a way that could be seen as patronising or demeaning. The ITC recognises that some stereotypes can be insulting to groups in question and that care is always needed not to condone or perpetuate prejudice. It therefore asked the hosts of two Chinese community internet discussion groups (which had debated the commercial) for their views. The hosts told the ITC that the use of genuine Cantonese speech went a long way to counter any potential for offence because it showed that the advertiser had thought carefully about how the theme of the advertisement was presented. The ITC understood how some might have found the advertisement objectionable. However, there had been no intention to mock and the ITC agreed that martial arts films were a significant part of Chinese culture and this advertisement had not depicted the culture or people in a negative light. It noted that the advertiser's employment of a language coach and translator had been recognised by those who had debated it via the internet discussion group to have been a commitment to ensuring that their language was accurately spoken.

CONCLUSION: Complaints not upheld.

TERMINAL TRITT

SIX

16 Sinclair Gardens,
London
W14 0AT

Gordon Ramsay,
Gordon Ramsay,
68-69 Royal Hospital Road,
London
SW3

17th January, 2000

Hey Arsehole! Why don't you fuck off home!

Only kidding Gordon! I loved your cookery series on TV last year and just thought I'd write in to see whether you have any plans to do another. I think you definitely should as you are easily the funniest out of Keith Floyd, who is a bit past it now, and Ainsley and the fat lady who has just died. I used to love it when you started shouting and swearing at all the chefs if they couldn't cook that funny food properly. Especially when they were foreigners.

Actually I've just read an article about your restaurant and I didn't realise how successful it was. I suppose there is a lot of money to be made serving up those small portions, and the people you have in like Joan Collins don't seem to care how much they pay for things anyway so it couldn't be better. My wife and I would like to come one night just to see what it's like, but I expect we'd have a job getting a table seeing as we are not famous and apparently you are always fully booked.

Do you do signed photos now that you are a celebrity yourself? I've sent an SAE if you do that would be great. Could you write something like fuck off or arsehole on it for me for a joke?

Thanks Gordon. Hope to see you back on TV again soon you big twat!

Best wishes,

Ralph Tritt

16 Sinclair Gardens,
London
W14 0AT

Doctor Fox,
Pepsi Chart Show,
Channel 5,
22 Long Acre,
London
WC2E 9LY

16th May, 2000

Dear Doctor Fox,

I wonder if you could give me the benefit of your advice with regard to some fashion tips?

I have recently taken early retirement but am still active and only in my fifties. My nephew, however, seems to think that I have just stepped off the ark and finds the way I dress a constant source of amusement. I have caught glimpses of your pop show on Channel 5 and for an oldie like myself you still seem in touch with the youngsters. What could you recommend for my wardrobe? Is there a special shop that you go to? I refuse to wear all this sports stuff covered in advertising and apparently even denims are out of fashion now.

I hope you don't mind me asking you this but even my wife thinks you look trendy. There is obviously a thin line between not dressing your age and looking ridiculous that you seem to have mastered.

Yours sincerely,

Ralph Tritt

16 Sinclair Gardens,
London
W14 0AT

A & R Department,
Bazal,
46-47 Bedford Square,
London
WC1B 3DP

13th September, 2000

Dear Sir/Madam,

I do hope that I have written to the right people or, if not, that you will be kind enough to point me in the proper direction.

I am planning to go on sale online with a number of gift items in time for the Christmas market, one of which being the Charlie Streamer© water feature. This is a reclining nude statuette of Ground Force's Charlie Dimmock cast in alloy which, when activated, projects a gush of water from an aperture in the crotch. My concern is that there may be some sort of copyright infringement here over the use of Ms. Dimmock's likeness and I do not want to start mass production only to become embroiled in litigation at some later stage.

Please let me know your feelings on this. If there is an issue, I do hope that it is something we can resolve quickly and easily. As you can imagine, this is a particularly strong product idea and one I expect to do very well with.

Thank you for your help.

Yours faithfully,

Ralph Tritt

272

16 Sinclair Gardens,
London
W14 0AT

3am,
Daily Mirror,
1 Canada Square,
Canary Wharf,
London
E14 5AP

7th December, 2000

Dear Girls,

It's only just occurred to me what a wicked wheeze your Wicked Whispers are! Here we all are, racking our brains trying to think who the blonde soap bitch is and the bald actor who likes amputees, and all the time you're just making them up!

It's a great idea for a space-filler, I have to say. Here are some that I have thought up myself. You can use them if you like.

• Who's the TV game show host who wears an Arab strap under his leather trousers?

• Which female DJ's kinky cocaine abuse wore a hole through her perineum?

• Who's the middle-aged soap star who caused a stink in a top London eaterie when he inadvertently sat on his own colostomy bag?

You may also like to know for your columns that I have recently spotted someone famous, BBC London Live DJ Gideon Coe. I saw him being intimate with a blonde woman (not his wife!) at the trendy Kensington foodie pub The Priory. They ordered vegetarian pasta and drank two bottles of house red.

All the best,

Ralph Tritt

16 Sinclair Gardens,
London
W14 0AT

Oz Clarke,
Food And Drink,
BBC Television Centre,
Wood Lane
London
W12

19th February, 2001

Dear Oz,

Any chance of a signed photo? I've enclosed an SAE for your trouble if you could oblige.

My wife Frances and I are both big fans of the programme and its lack of airs and graces. In fact she refers to you and AWT as the Odd Couple! (You don't really live in his shed, do you? That's weird!) Actually, he does seem to throw his weight around a bit, even though he has to stand on a piece of tupperware. Is it true what they say about Jilly Goolden having to leave the show? I know that she's only small too, but we heard she got carried away with the tasting and would become difficult to handle. Apparently she's a filthy tongue on her after a couple as well. And she looks like butter wouldn't melt!

Finally Oz, could you settle a dispute for us? My wife insists that you started out as an actor in Z Cars but I say you'd be far more likely to have a background in retail. Who's right?

Happy tippling Oz, but don't end up like Jilly! Best regards to AWT.

Yours sincerely,

Ralph Tritt

16 Sinclair Gardens,
London
W14 0AT

Tony Banks MP,
House Of Commons,
Westminster,
London
SW1

3rd May, 2001

Dear Mr. Banks,

I am glad to see that you have taken up cudgels with regard to mayor Ken Livingstone's outrageous decision to outlaw the sale of bird food in Trafalgar Square. I don't have to tell you that the consequences of this mindless action really don't bear thinking about. Quite apart from jeopardizing the lives of countless pigeons, London will end up being deprived of one of its most distinctive and well-loved sights.

My wife and I have already decided that direct action is called for and to this end are relocating birds to Shepherd's Bush Green and Holland Park where we know there is food aplenty. If Trafalgar Square is to lose its pigeons, we see no reason why they should be lost to London as a whole. We know that the birds are far from stupid and have strong navigational instincts. It is our hope that the ones we successfully transfer will remember where they are should they fly back, and perhaps lead others when they return.

We transfer the birds a brace at a time in cardboard cat boxes available from any pet shop, but with an estimated 40,000 in the Square it is, of course, a hopeless task. I propose that you call upon fellow Londoners to follow suit and give your blessing to a relocation programme. That way we could have pigeons redistributed throughout the parks and green belts of London quickly and evenly. It would secure their future as well as being one in the eye for Livingstone! Food for thought.

Keep up the good work. We shall.

Yours sincerely,

Ralph And Frances Tritt
(Bird Lovers)

275

16 Sinclair Gardens,
London
W14 0AT

The Secretary,
British Non-Ferrous Metals Federation,
6 Bathurst Street,
Sussex Square,
London
W2

9th May, 2001

Dear Sir,

I would be most interested to receive information with a view to joining the Federation and enclose a large SAE for your convenience.

I would also like to disclose at this juncture an earlier affiliation with the Iron And Steel Trades Confederation and trust that this will not prejudice you against me in any way.

Yours faithfully,

Ralph Tritt

16 Sinclair Gardens,
London
W14 0AT

Director Of Marketing,
Warner-Lambert Consumer Healthcare,
Lambert Court,
Chestnut Avenue,
Eastleigh,
Hants
SO5 3ZQ

5th July, 2001

Dear Sir/Madam,

I am the manager of a unique variety act, The Gargling Patels. I am, at present, considering a number of offers for professional representation with a view to making a significant impact in the entertainment industry.

Given the specialised nature of the act (close harmony vocalising with liquid) and potential cross-cultural appeal, it has struck me that an exciting branding/marketing opportunity could exist here for your product, Listerine. The troupe (a family of six) currently use bottled water for their routine.

I can't pretend to know anything about striking sponsorship deals, being new to this side of the business. What I do know, however, it that you are not about to start chucking money at a concept with no profile. But what if we were to use Listerine exclusively for the act and have your logo displayed prominently on the national costumes? Surely that would be worth parting with a little free stock to begin with? It may also interest you to know that Jamal and Rita Patel run their own mini-market when not performing.

These are early days, and it could be that our agent (when chosen) will be the one to do the bidding and not myself. I am keen, however, in the meantime, to take a few soundings in an attempt to guage whether this is something that you would like to be a part of (either now or at a later stage) and, if so, to what extent.

Yours faithfully,

Ralph Tritt

16 Sinclair Gardens,
London
W14 0AT

Paul Dacre,
Editor,
Daily Mail,
Northcliffe House,
2 Derry Street,
London
W8 5TT

7th November, 2001

Dear Mr. Dacre,

Just a few lines of praise with regard to today's issue.

Like a lot of male readers, I look forward to your nude celebrity features with some relish. (Why not make it a weekly thing?) Gwyneth Paltrow, though, will have to take some beating! Who ever would have thought she'd been blessed with a seat like that? She looks like a stick with her clothes on! It's no good, there's only one word for it: Phooarrh!

I also found the J. K. Rowling article revealing but in a different way. Catching her like that with her provocative underwear purchases just goes to show that it takes more than a big bank account to satisfy a younger partner in the bedroom. Even for her.

Anyway, keep up the good work. If you're taking requests, how about Mariella Frostrup in the buff? I've a feeling her seat might just eclipse Ms. Paltrow's full moon!

Yours sincerely,

Ralph Tritt

278

16 Sinclair Gardens,
London
W14 0AT

Alison Boshoff,
Showbusiness Editor,
Daily Mail,
Northcliffe House,
2 Derry Street,
London
W8 5TT

10th January, 2002

Dear Ms. Boshoff,

It's always good to see something about Madonna (the Material Girl!) in the newspaper, but I think you have drawn the wrong conclusion in your recent article "From Glam To Glum".

The photograph of her looking plain while out shopping on the Fulham Road suggests, you say, a depressed state, and you make the comparison with another photograph taken at an awards ceremony to prove your point. If you don't mind me saying, I think you are confusing the public and the private sides of Madonna's life. By dressing down, I think you will find she is just trying to avoid being recognised in the street. Certainly her going out in full make-up and low-cut bra would cause all manner of unwanted attention, quite apart from being severely impractical given the weather!

Otherwise, do keep up the good work. Your showbiz tit-bits are a pleasant enough distraction.

Yours sincerely,

Ralph Tritt

16 Sinclair Gardens,
London
W14 0AT

Clarissa Dickson Wright,
BBC Scotland,
Queen Margaret Drive,
Glasgow
G12 8DG

22nd January, 2002

Dear Mrs. Dickson Wright,

My wife and I were both saddened by the death of your fat friend and thought we'd seen the last of you on the box. It's good to see that you still have a career in television without her.

I have to say, though, that I much preferred it when you were cooking. This Johnny chap you have on now seems to have a high opinion of himself and treats you like some sort of stooge. All he does is go on about vermin and dogs and how to fix a fence. It's not exactly entertainment. I think you'd be better off taking control in the kitchen again and showing us some more of your farm house specials with him as the side-kick. Plenty of offal and pastry, no nonsense food I call it.

Would it be rude to ask where you get your trousers? My wife, Frances, is a big woman too, but can't seem to find anything other than leggings that will go up over her pot. You seem to manage all right with yours and cut quite a dash in them. Were they specially made for the series?

I've enclosed an SAE for a signed photo if you could oblige. Good luck for the future, but not with old Johnny. You look as though you could have him for breakfast so perhaps you should.

Yours sincerely,

Ralph Tritt

TRITT COMESTIBLES
"No Nonsense Catering"
16 Sinclair Gardens, West Kensington, London W14 0AT

American Peanut Council,
Grosvenor Gardens House,
Grosvenor Gardens,
London
SW1

31st January, 2002

Dear Sirs,

I am a small, independent catering enterprise, always keen to diversify and embrace fresh business opportunities. After dabbling recently with turkey, I am now giving serious thought to nuts as my next venture.

I am wondering whether you can put me straight on your function. Are you concerned solely with the representation of American nuts in this country by other Americans, or are the nuts you bandy available to all? I ask as one concerned with bulk purchase, providing the logistics can be realised.

If you are merely a group of nut enthusiasts, could you point me in the direction of someone who deals in the commodity, American or otherwise?

I look forward to hearing from you.

Yours faithfully,

Ralph Tritt
MANAGING DIRECTOR

281

EPILOGUE

432B Kings Rd
London SW10 0LJ

19 January, 2000

MI5 Counter Espionage Dept
Albert Embankment
London SE1

Dear Sirs,

I wish to report a possible spy. Mrs Tritt a colleague of mine at the Grey Foxes Senior Theatre Society, has expressed the notion that 'all men are equal' and apparently plans a visit to Prague in the autumn. She may be found in rented rooms at 16 Sinclair Gardens W8.

This is very sensitive information, please treat it with care, I do not wish to 'terminated' with a Bulgarian umbrella.

Yours Sincerely

Perry Edgbaston

PO BOX 3255
LONDON
SW1P 1AE

Mr P Edgbaston
432B Kings Road
London
SW10 0LJ

31 January 2000

Dear Mr Edgbaston

Thank you for your letter of 19 January 2000.

Yours sincerely,

T. Denham
for the Director General